Tallahassee Writers Association

SEVEN HILLS REVIEW
2022

Tallahassee Writers Association

SEVEN HILLS REVIEW
2022

Volume 27

turtle cove press

Tallahassee, Florida

ISBN: 978-1-947536-13-5
Library of Congress Control Number: 2022930666

Managing Editor: M.R. Street, MPH, MSI
Copy Editor: Liz Jameson, https://editedbyliz.com/
Cover Photo © M.R. Street 2021

Dedicated to the memory of
Peggy Kassees
1952 - 2022

Previous issues of the *Seven Hills Review* may be purchased at Amazon.com.

Other titles published by Turtle Cove Press are available at **https://www.turtlecovepress.com**.

Foreword

The Seven Hills Literary Contest and Penumbra Poetry and Haiku Contest is an annual project of the Tallahassee Writers Association. All entry screening, reader reviews, manuscript preparation, artwork, publishing, and other contributions are volunteer efforts of the Tallahassee Writers Association.

First, second, and third place winners in each category receive a cash prize and are published in the following year's *Seven Hills Review* anthology. First place winners also receive a complimentary copy of the *Seven Hills Review.*

The decision of which categories to include in the contest is made each year prior to the contest opening for entries. This year, we added a new category: Personal Essay. Unfortunately, at the conclusion of the contest, the contest committee decided to eliminate the 10-Minute Play category due to insufficient responses.

The contest received 104 entries from authors who hail from 14 states, France, and the Philippines. We are excited that the Seven Hills Contest continues to receive international interest.

To our winning authors, CONGRATULATIONS! And to all our submitters, thank you for writing, polishing, and submitting your work. We hope you participate again next year! For the latest information on entering and entry criteria, be sure to check for updates at **https://twaonline.org/.**

A final note: If you are not already a member of Tallahassee Writers Association, please consider joining. You can check out the benefits of membership at: **https://twaonline.org/.**

Contents

*Erratum

Kathy Lippard Cobb's Haiku, *Stone Roses,* received an honorable mention in the 2016 Seven Hills Contest. Unfortunately, it was incorrectly attributed to a different author in the Table of Contents of the 2017 *Seven Hills Review.* We apologize for this error, and are reprinting Kathy's Haiku–with proper attribution–in this edition of the Seven *Hills Review.*

The Judging Process

Judging is a three-step process. First, entries are vetted by the Contest Committee to determine whether they meet the eligibility requirements and to scrub any personal data on the entry itself or in the file properties prior to reader review. The rules are posted online, and should be adhered to rigorously. This is good training for authors, who must follow submission guidelines when submitting to literary agents and publishers. All judging is blind; we have to ensure that no preference is shown to submitters known to our readers or judges.

The second step involves a cadre of readers. Our readers are volunteers who donated countless hours reading through the submissions in their categories. At least three readers read each entry and assign scores of yes (+1), maybe (0), or no (-1). Scores are averaged to minimize the bias of personal preference. Readers, without you, we couldn't begin to assess all the entries! We thank you heartily!

The third step in the process is review by the category judges. The judges provide their expertise with no compensation other than a complimentary copy of the anthology. The top-scoring entries in each category are sent to the category judge. The judges are respected, published authors in their respective categories. Each judge used a genre-specific set of criteria to score the top entries in their category. Judges are also given freedom to add points to any entry that exhibited intangible qualities that made it rise above the others. Judges, we thank you all for your professionalism and for donating your expert services to the production of this anthology.

To everyone who reads this volume, we hope you enjoy the winning selections. Congratulations to all our winners.

THE SEVEN HILLS
LITERARY COMPETITION

Flash Fiction
Final Judge — Anna Yeatts
Pinehurst, North Carolina

First Place
Aftermath
Lyla Ellzey
Tallahassee, Florida

They came together, these Covid-haunted survivors. They wore their face masks, glasses clouding with their ragged breaths. They maintained social distance and, with gloved hands, yearned for another's touch.

"What did 2020 mean to us?" one asked, dripping sanitizer into her palm.

"Perhaps it meant the same to all," another uttered, eyeing the distance between them.

"I know; let's say one word to describe what 2020 meant to each of us," a third voiced.

"I bet they will be similar," a fourth opined.

"Let's do it!" they all said, excitement muffled behind the confining face shields.

"Miserable," she said.

"Blessed," said he.

"Awful," he said.

"Happy," said she.

"Sorrow," she said.

"Joy," said he.

"Stressful," he said.

"Peace," said she.

"Draining," she said.

"Journey," said he.

"Toxic," he said.

"Perseverance," said she.

"Hell," she said.

"Interesting," said he.

"Deadly," he said.

"Forward," said she.

"Horrible," she said.

"Promise," said he.

"About half of us viewed 2020 negatively," one began.

"And about half of us viewed 2020 positively," another pointed out.

"What one word describes our feelings about 2021?" a third asked.

A mighty roar arose from the throats of those gathered: "HOPE!" The word flew above them, out the opened window, and floated on the rising wind toward the heavens. "HOPE! HOPE!"

A being greater than the mere mortals who shouted it heard that word: "HOPE!" The being lifted it from the currents, tucked it close, and thundered, "2021 shall be a year of HOPE!"

"HOPE triumphs over uncertainty and brings calming rest, so sorely needed for mankind's future," IT stated.

"HOPE!" again roared the masses.

"And so it shall be," IT declared.

And so it was.

So be it.

Second Place
His Way
Richard Key
Dothan, Alabama

"How's Kelley taking your diagnosis?"

"She says I'm stupid," said Vince, looking up at his wife as she re-entered the room where we were sitting, bringing back the tray I'd brought their dinner on.

"I did not say you were stupid. What I said was you did things your way, which is to wait and wait and procrastinate until things are way more serious. That's your way, Vince. That's all I said. And that's the stupid way."

"Same difference. Some wives are supportive."

"Some wives suggest that their husbands have a check-up, and their husband actually goes. Some wives spend hours searching for a specialist with the expectation that he will have enough sense to seek help before it's too late."

"I did go."

"Yes, you did go. That you did. You get one point for going. And minus ten for waiting till you lost twenty pounds and turned yellow."

I was caught in the crossfire, and mentally tried to shrink myself, but then Kelley turned to me as she continued to rant: "The problem, it turns out, is not cancer. It's mule-headedness. That's the disease and there's no cure for that. What good is modern medicine if you're imprisoned by your foolish male pride?"

Finally, she looked away from me and gazed out the window.

"I'm trying to get past my anger, and when I do, I'll be

supportive," she said. "Maybe I can take a day off from work and we can shop for caskets together."

"Well, I'd better be off," I said, rising from my seat, tray in hand, hoping to slink away before anything else exploded.

"Don't go," Vince said, grabbing me by the sleeve. "Protect me."

"Then we can go pick out a headstone. It'll say: Here lies Vince Davidson (singing) *He did it his way.*"

I did manage to leave, Vince holding his pathetic arms out to me like a weary two-year-old.

***

I followed Vince's decline on Facebook, posting a thumbs up if there was a tiny shred of good news or a caring emoji if the news was not very encouraging. I was a bald-faced coward. I admit it. It wasn't hard to find some reason not to visit my old friend from college days.

As it turned out, I didn't see him again for six weeks, this time at the funeral home. Vince was dressed up in his finest grey suit, but otherwise looked about the same. He was standing beside Kelley's casket where she reposed, arms crossed with a single rose.

"I sure am sorry, pal," I told him. "When I heard about the accident, I couldn't believe it."

"Yeah," he answered. "When it rains it pours."

"Someone said the brakes failed?"

"That's what they think," he said. "The mechanic warned me they needed replacing, but I just kept putting it off."

I tried to forget what I heard next. "Maybe I'm not so stupid after all."

Short Stories
Final Judge — Lyla Ellzey
Tallahassee, Florida

First Place
Dead Lakes Promise
Bruce Ballister
Tallahassee, Florida

"Daddy, why is that fog so thick?"

Jerrell Cobb looked up from a tackle box and followed his daughter's pointing finger. A solid wall of white was slowly moving toward them, eclipsing trees in moments as its leading edge swallowed each cypress, one by one. It was still a few hundred yards off on the other side of a slough. Its progress visible as each tree, in turn, faded to grey and disappeared.

The November afternoon had been forecast to get chilly, and they'd brought jackets for the eventuality, but the thin cloud cover had allowed plenty of light and warmth for them to fish and navigate the numerous channels in the western tributaries of the Apalachicola River known as the Dead Lakes. Jerrell looked back to his daughter who was looking up from her seat in the jon boat with simple curiosity. What to answer? Meteorology? Physics? His best guess beyond those obvious answers was an *I don't know*. He went with meteorology. "Hun, it's a cold front moving in. You remember I told you to bring your jacket in case it got colder while we were still out here." He pointed. "Well, there it is."

He stared at the advancing wall, then over his shoulder at the still barely visible sun. Its final warmth of the day died as it and its colorful ice rings in bars of high cirrus slid behind lower stratus. "Go ahead and put that jacket on, honey." A glance at the inexorable approach of the fog sent a chill through him that had nothing to do with the temperature.

"But that's a very strange fog," she said. "I thought they were wispy, like sitting inside a cloud."

"True, but we're looking at the fog from the outside."

She looked up at him. "I think I remember why there's fog."

"Ok, give it a shot." Michelina was bright and took to reading early. He'd been impressed when, several years back, she'd rescued an aging *World Book Encyclopedia* set from a neighbor's garage sale for ten dollars. At odd moments, he would find her simply reading the picture filled books from start to finish. She knew a lot.

Michelina looked over at the fog, seeming to see if what she saw fit her knowledge. "Well, it's November and the swamp water is still warm. But really cold air is coming now, and cold air over warm water makes for fog. That's what makes the Grand Banks off Massachusetts so dangerous; the Gulf Stream carries warm water from Florida up north where it meets cold air and covers the fishing grounds with fog."

"Very good. Impressive." The line of grey was almost upon them now. He reached for his own jacket as his daughter was stretching into hers. As he lifted his from the seat beside him, there was a soft plop in the dark tannic water. Too late, he saw the glowing rectangle of his cell phone fading in the brown stained waters of Dead Lakes. He didn't muffle the "Aw, sh—!" nearly enough and looked up to see her eyes widen with understanding.

"Your phone's still in the shop, right?" he asked.

His question was answered with a sluggish nod. Her face began to wrinkle, transitioning from frown to tearful.

"Mich, we're going to be OK. Don't worry, people are all over these swamps fishing today." With pride, he watched her hitch her breathing up, swallow a sob, and dab at her eyes with the cuff of her jacket. He wished he had the confidence she'd just shown. With his phone, he could have at least navigated and worked his way through the complicated feeders that separated the small town of Wewahitchka and Hwy 71 from the main channel of the river to the East. Without it, Wewa, as anyone from the surrounding counties called it, was almost anywhere. His last understanding of which channel led home might be somewhere ahead.

In the next hour, they moved slowly between apparent channels, amid thick groves of young cypress, hammocks of sweet gum, titi thickets, and ancient husks of dead trees. Time after time, they'd found a choke point where their hoped-for road to home disappeared into a thicket of trees and deadfall. The white soup thinned now and then but took on darker shades of grey as first the overcast shaded the fog and then the lowering sun robbed the grey wisps of light.

"Sweetie, go ahead and eat that leftover sandwich. I'm sure we'll find our way out of this pretty soon." His own optimism may have shaded the delivery, but Michelina's gusto while devouring the last of their wax paper wrapped sandwiches didn't seem to be deflated. He'd motored into and backed out of too many cuts in the tree line. On occasion, he'd hear a vehicle honk, or motor noise, but the thick blanket of fog dampened any hope of direction finding.

Darkness was going to find them, before they found safety.

In the bottom of his tacklebox, Jerrell found the small tach light he used to help on night excursions. Usually, he held the small penlight in his mouth while retying a swivel or baiting a cricket. It was all he had; his boat wasn't equipped for night running. Hearing motor noise, he turned behind to feel, or rather, sense a moving outboard some distance behind them. It was moving from his right to left as he peered over his seven-and-a-half Johnson into the darkening gloom.

"Hey! Hey!" He shouted, then they shouted toward the noise. "Help us!" In variations and in turn, they shouted at the passing boat to no avail. The fog swallowed its soft purring in less than two minutes, and they were alone again in the thick, grey soup. He backed and turned, looking for the channel the other boater had found. The best option was in following a small oil slick Any residual boil in the water from the passing motor had been quickly dampened by the nearly complete cover of lily pads. Too soon, any evidence of the slick dissipated. He cut his motor and listened.

Silence. Silence deeper than a cave's quiet settled over the dead lakes as even the birds and critters paused their evening ritual in silent observance of the darkening blanket of too-thick fog. He heard only his tinnitus, a thin whine at almost dog-whistle frequency. He looked into the hopeful face of his first born, Michelina Cobb. Twelve years old, going on twenty-one. Such an amazing child. "Girl? We are in a pickle; I won't sugar coat it. I think we are in or near a main channel. Without the phone, I can't find us on a map. I can't get a good fix on which of these sloughs gets us back to the landing, or anyone's back yard even."

"Daddy, I'm not scared."

"Not even a little? It would be OK. I might be if I was your age."

"Look, we're in a perfectly good boat." She tapped the gunnel with pride, then looked down at the red plastic gas can's float gauge. "We have half a tank of gas. And we have sushi for dinner. If it comes to that."

"Sushi?"

In the gloom he could barely make out her face, but it seemed to pucker a little. "I never had catfish sushi, or bass sushi, but I'd try it before I starved."

She joined in as he laughed out loud. "Bass sushi, four dollars apiece, twelve dollars for the roll."

She countered with, "Catfish sushi rolls, fresh as it gets, come and get it."

They laughed until his belly hurt. As if hearing the chorus, splashing in the wet well brought them back to their condition. "So, my dear," he said, "I think the best thing to do, at least until this edge of the front moves past, is to sit tight. Save this little flashlight for signaling and see if another boat comes by or if anyone comes looking."

"We could keep fishing," she offered.

"That we could." As the dark grey turned to black, they set cricket and bobber lines out and waited.

Time wore slowly, and the gloom finally revealed stars overhead and a thin crescent moon to what he assumed was west based on his own thin knowledge of astronomy. Knowing what was west and knowing how to get west to the landing were two different things. The fog was now only a few feet thick. He proved this and stood above it, marveling at the soft carpet of white that seemed to provide a snowscape never before seen in the Dead Lakes.

"Sweetheart, stand up on the seat and look at this. Careful, don't rock us."

His daughter stood and turned to take in the starlit scene. She caught site of the crescent moon and pointed. "Lookit, Dad.

That looks like the moon from the movie logo. There could be a kid sitting in the crook and dropping a fishing line."

Despite the cold, his smile warmed his heart. He was so proud of this little girl. No, this young lady. She was wise beyond her years. Doing everything beyond his expectations to keep herself and him calm.

"Daddy? What do you suppose that kid in the moon is fishing for?"

"I don't know. Maybe he's fishing for new ideas for movies."

Her laugh rang out across the now-clearing but dimly-lit scene. He didn't want to shine his little light out into the darkness because he knew there would be plenty of evidence that they were not alone. Gators, usually circumspect and all but concealed in daylight would be on the prowl. Even seeing the number of orange eyes in the night could easily frighten the still buoyant spirits of his girl.

"You know," she started, "if I was fishing for ideas…" the pause lingered. "Yes?"

"If I was fishing for ideas, I'd work on how to make humans better people."

"And do you have any? Ideas on how to do that?"

"First we'd have to figure out how to unwrite some of the meanness in some folks. Some folks are just mean. Plenty of good ones too. For sure. But the mean ones seem to get to be in charge."

"OK, so we work on mean people. I agree, too many of them do get to be in charge, mostly, I suppose because good people didn't want to offend them, or they just bullied their way in. I get that. Any more?"

She was putting tension on her line, testing to see if anything was on the other end. Bait or fish. She let the line go slack again.

"There's too many people hungry too. We'd have to make a law or something that no one could go hungry, that it was against the law. Corporations would get fined if the things they did made it hard for poor folks to get a chance at a square meal."

"That's quite an idea you've got on that hook. I—"

"Really quite simple, Dad. There's plenty of lawyers busy now with mean people. If they weren't busy in the courts, they can work on the laws we'd need."

He nodded thoughtfully in the dark. "Okay, so you're gonna save the world by getting rid of meanness and hunger. That's quite an agenda. That ought to keep you busy for a lifetime if you could work on either of those…."

"But," she interrupted, "then there's war. As I see it. For the longest time, this country, and other countries all over have been at war. Over what?"

"Well—" He paused, scratched at his chin in the dark.

"They've been fighting because it gets mean people in power, and when they get to be in power, they have to be at war with somebody to stay in power."

"Whoa! That's a lot! World peace?" His heart grew a size with pride. "Just a minute, I'm thinking."

Jerrell sat back a bit, amazed at her understanding of the basic fundamental commonality.

So many regimes around the world depended upon an "Us vs. Them" media stream to hold a population at bay, to raise money for arms, to keep the peace at a local level.

Michelina started slowly, "What starts war is politics, religion, fuel, and food right?" In the moonlit gloom, he could see her ticking off the list on her fingers. The Germans used politics, religion, and lies to blame all their troubles on the Jews and anyone else and killed millions of people. And all over

Africa there's tribes and countries fighting over food. Right?"

"Yes."

"And the Japanese started war on their side of the world because they needed fuel to become a big power. Right?"

"Yes again."

And then, "So, it's simple."

He looked into her hard gaze. The thin slice of moonlight put a tiny spark in her eyes. She had in a few sentences gotten to the bottom of suffering for millions upon millions. But he was hooked by her final assumption. "What's simple about all of that?"

"There's too many humans."

"Oh my, honey, that's going to be a hard one to fix."

"Well, I know. But if we could stop war all over the world by having fewer babies, how in the world do you make that happen?"

"Education. So, you want to be a teacher?"

"No." She nodded over his shoulder at the crescent moon. It was almost lost in the black-on-black profile of the cypress and gum trees surrounding them. "I think I want to make movies."

"That's very possible. And an honorable profession, especially if you want to do it to inform, to teach." He was about to expand on it when he subliminally felt then saw a flashing red strobing the trunks beyond. Over his shoulder, he caught a flash of red against trees, and then heard the motor. He quickly got his tach light out and began to wave it left and right in the direction of the approaching boat.

By 1:00 a.m., they were at the landing at the Dead Lakes Bridge over Hwy 71. They'd been able to call home thanks to a deputy's phone, and all would be well. Hot chocolate and hot coffee helped warm the chill in their bones. As the deputies finished their loading, father and daughter turned toward their truck. He slowed and put his hand on her shoulder. "Michelina?"

The tired response came, "Yeah Dad?"

He could see the last glimmer of the moon, shining in her eyes. "I don't know how to tell you how proud I am of you. A lot of people, a lot of kids your age might have been very scared to be out in that place, with all those gators, in that fog, that creepy fog."

She curled into him, her arms around his chest. Soon, he thought, she'd be taller than her mother. He felt her hug hard on his ribs, it felt harder than usual, and he hugged back, just as hard. He leaned down and kissed the top of her head. "Come on, we need to get home. Your mother is going to be a nervous wreck."

As they sat in the car, she reached over and touched his hand before he could turn the keys. "Thank you, Daddy."

He turned to see tears streaming down her cheeks in the light of the dashboard. "Honey, it's OK, we're safe now. We'll be home in a few hours."

"No, I mean, thank you. I think I know what I'm going to do. With my life." He took his hand away from the ignition and held her hand, returned a squeeze.

He heard a slight catch in her breath before she continued. "I hope this is a promise I can make to myself, something I will always remember as the why. This night, that fog, and that crescent moon."

He patted her head, smiling in and out, turned the key and headed the car north, toward home. Thirty minutes later, in the light of the next town up the road, he looked over to see the sleeping form of the greatest new filmmaker of two decades from now. His Christmas list now revised to include a decent digital video camera and software. He'd do what he could to keep her promise to herself. Changing the world was a worthy enough cause.

Second Place
The Purse
Bruce Ballister
Tallahassee, Florida

Billy walked further down the alley. Smells of leftovers filled the darkness, mocking his hunger. Club music faded as he put distance between himself and the street. He wasn't much to look at any more. The city had removed most of his sensibility, and now the city was finishing off whatever was left. He reached his box behind a stack of palettes and prepared it for the night. Crawling inside, he lit a flashlight against the darkness and perused the contents of the bag he'd just snatched.

She'd been too easy. Billy wondered if she was a tourist from the heartland or just stupid. Nobody walked around with a long-strapped purse anymore and didn't strap it around their neck. It had been a simple bump in the crowd. She had been pretty too. He looked first for the driver's license to see who she was and to look again into the eyes that had been so startled.

Out of the main pouch he dumped essential cosmetics, a deck of credit cards, phone, keys, a can of mace. A heavy base beat overlaid by Japanese techno-pop filtered down the alleyway from the club out on the street. Someone opened a side door. A light had come on at the back door of the nightclub. The music boomed into the alley. He quickly turned out his flashlight and listened. The side door of the dumpster across the alley slid open with a reverberating metallic bang followed by sounds of garbage being thrown in. The dumpster door slammed shut with a hollow steel wham and footsteps retreated to the club door. After some muffled conversation, the music retreated too, leaving only a thumping base beat that pulsed through the walls and pavement.

Billy thought a little about the beat. Was his heart actually in sync with the tempo? Was he just being melodramatic? Flashlight on, he resumed his desperate search of the little leather purse. Actually, it was more of a hand bag with a strap, not much capacity. He had taken some that were large enough to use for groceries. *Damn!* No driver's license. Maybe she carried that in a jacket pocket or something. She sure had been pretty though, that was why he had started walking beside her, and she had been staring at him earlier. Blonde, retro, preppy, she had one of those faux school jackets and a white blouse with a navy skirt. So very fifties.

He unzipped the side pocket and upturned the purse onto the floor of the box to comb through the stolen pieces of a stranger's life. A half-used roll of mints, two keys on a ring, a Saint Christopher medallion and chain, and a really neat little turquoise carving. A few small coins, a few more crumpled receipts, and dirt ended the stream of miscellany. No license. He did find an employee badge from one of the cellphone companies with a mag strip on the back. *Wonder if that's an access swipe strip?*

He looked again at the front of the badge. Sally Owens. He looked again at the picture. The face on the ID badge was a blonde but about twenty-five pounds heavier than his mark. She looked vaguely familiar, but she looked like a lot of people. He had always had the theory that there were only so many faces possible to humanity and they were repeated at random throughout the gene pool. A final count revealed that he had a little over sixty-seven dollars in cash and a bank card that could be useful if he could find a pin somewhere. Not a bad grab. He decided to look for a pin number on the paper scraps in the morning. In the little pile he found the overlooked driver's license and verified the name and the formerly heavier face. Its date had expired. He did the math on the birth date. Sally was 32.

He looked again at the turquoise trinket. It was oval and nearly flat on one side. The front had a shallow relief symbol of some kind he'd seen somewhere before. It didn't look Indian, and it didn't look oriental. The inscription carved on the flat side was too small to read in the dim light of the flashlight. He thought the symbol must have some significance beyond just being a simple design, but he couldn't think of it.

He was finally tired enough to sleep, but he had to see what had just been thrown in the dumpster. He wanted to get at any food before it went bad. Billy slid out of the bottom of the triple weight refrigerator box, a great find, and checked around the corner of the wall that shielded his hideaway from the street. Seeing no action coming his way, he crossed over to the dumpster and reached to slide open the trash door.

There she was! Standing at the end of the alley; between glances into his darkness, she was looking at something out of his sight and talking. "*Sh—! She must have followed me back here.*" He stood absolutely still wondering how much she could see in the darkness of the alley. He certainly couldn't risk the noises of the metal bin. Even over the music from the club, there would be clanging. Hell, she had followed him all the way back here. For sixty-seven dollars? She must be crazy. You could get killed in this neighborhood. Not that he had any intentions himself; it was just nuts to be here after dark if you weren't in groups or armed or both.

Street neon flashes illuminated her in surreal colors. He could see that she was still in the school-girl uniform, but the white blouse blinked between off-yellow and pink with the pulsing of the nightclub's marquee lights. She walked to one side and out of sight but immediately returned. She paced as she held up a cell phone and began to talk into it. She rarely took her eyes off the darkened depth of the alley as she talked and even gestured into it as she spoke. He was transfixed. He was busted.

She had looked so sweet and innocent, naive even. But she must have gotten up after the shove, caught the direction of his departure, picked up on his double back and stayed with him through the several moves that he thought were cleverly designed to confuse a tail if he were followed. Getting on and off the trolley was the simplest and usually most effective method of diluting his trail with crowds. But damn, there she was, and he was busted. He slid farther back into shadow.

Billy noticed a new smell in the alley. It was him. Even over the stench of the garbage and his own B.O. he could smell his fear. He didn't want to go back inside. He might get killed this time. Just thirty days for vagrancy and petty theft could get him beat up or much worse in a Frisco jail. Funny how cops didn't react to screams when they were coming from jail cells. He rubbed his hands on the filthy walls of the building next to him and darkened the backs of his hands. Repeating the motion, he darkened his face.

No, he thought, *that's just stupid*. With some bravado built out of desperation he slowly returned to the hidden corner that contained his tiny cardboard world. He grabbed the ID card, the cash, and the green amulet and peered around the corner toward the end of the alley. She was still there. He looked around again to verify that there were no ladders, windows or loosened doors that he could disappear into. Man, he hated this. Sixty-seven dollars, well.

He returned to the box and gathered up the little bits of make-up and trivia. He even reached to the deep end of the box and retrieved the mints minus one. Chewing that one, he faced the worst of his fears and walked into the light. The techno pop background track had been alternating between a thin female rap and keyboard riffs. He thought to rub some of the dirt from his face. The woman, Sally, could see him now and quit pacing. He affected a limp to look more pitiful and more or less dragged his left foot until he was within 30 feet of her. He then remembered that she had seen him run from her earlier in the night and dropped the ruse.

She watched him as he emerged from the dark, shadowed alley. He was removing things from his jacket pocket and putting them back into her purse. He stopped about twenty feet away and was looking both foolish and uneasy. Looking more at the ground than at her, he started patting his pockets for any more of the purse's contents. He stopped the searching and his body visibly sagged. With as little self-respect as a human could display and still be motile, Billy approached her.

"It's all here, miss. I'm so sorry if I scared you and all." He wiped his mouth with the back of his hand. "For those of you with a life, it must be hard to think about us...." He stopped. He didn't look up at her. "I'm sorry I took your purse." He said again, "If you don't mind, I kept twenty dollars, but please don't call the cops. I get so hungry." Billy didn't bother to tell her about the breath mint. He took another few steps forward and held out his hand with the purse dangling from a fingertip. She held her hand out in acceptance but didn't enter into the alley from the sidewalk. He looked up at her, his eyes clearly frightened. "It's all here," he repeated. "Well, almost." He remembered that he had confessed to the twenty.

The young woman took a small step toward him and extended her arm. He watched the small black purse cross between them as if someone else's hand were offering it. The disconnected hand looped the strap over her outstretched fingers. Her relief was visible to any who might have chanced to see the exchange. Billy stepped back, just short of the shadow line from the street light. "I'm so sorry, I get so hungry."

"Stop it, just stop." Sally looked frustrated beyond herself. She looked up and down the street. No one to be worried about. She took a step forward into the alley. "Come on, Dad. Let me get you some dinner and maybe later, you'll come home tonight." He did not respond beyond dropping his chin to his chest. After a short pause, she added. "You do know who I am don't you? It's me, Sally."

He felt very confused, "No, Miss, uhm, Sally?" Vertigo was coming on now, space expanded, gravity thickened. His fear had melted into shame. A flood of thoughts that would not merge into coherency jumped in and out of his mind's eye, competing with the yellow and pink flashes from the night club's garish lights. The visions swirled, slowed, and whisked away. His left eye ticked, a tear tracked down his cheek to be slowed by a four-day stubble. Because of the rushing in his ears, he didn't hear the Buick drive up.

"Come on Dad, it's me, Sally. Ted is here now, and we can go eat something." She reached out. "You are hungry, aren't you?" A tall young man came to stand beside her, and then came over to him with a reassuring arm extended, palm up, empty. "Please, Pop!" She pleaded again, "You have to take your meds."

The voice was somehow familiar, and it was comforting, and he was very hungry. But, his daughter? *I have a daughter? Meds?*

He didn't know for sure, but he had been hungry too often and didn't like it. He let himself be guided into the back seat of the Buick, glad he had taken the breath mint. As the Buick started to roll forward, he glanced back at the alley, already missing his cardboard home and wondering if he'd be able to find it again.

Adult Novel Excerpt
Final Judge — Marina Brown
Tallahassee, Florida

First Place
The Real Story
James Christy
Princeton, New Jersey

Chapter 1: Flight

So I wake up in the men's bathroom in Terminal 2 of JFK airport. Maybe I should say come to. At the moment I come to I see that my flow is aimed about 2 feet to the left of a urinal, where the urinal divider meets the wall. I was grateful for the urinal divider, which I now understood was intended for this purpose. But quickly I saw that while it was working to a degree, as most of my urine was staying on my side of the divider, a significant amount of backsplash was landing on a light tan leather Samsonite just to my left. The owner of the Samsonite was a South Asian man, who was shouting and gesticulating at me in a lovely British accent, while trying to rescue the Samsonite from the line of fire.

I say trying because he himself appeared to be mid-flow and clearly was concerned about maintaining his own aim. He finished quickly, though, and was soon above me. I recall him being very tall, but I may have just been slouching as a protective measure. I didn't catch a lot of what he said, which was far more detailed and nuanced than you might expect for the situation. The gist was that his mother had given this Samsonite luggage set when he moved to America, and it had become for her a symbol of the family's mobility. And how was he supposed to enter her home with this luggage that would smell of my piss? I found a $20 bill in my pocket, one of my last, and held it out to him, my hand shaking. He looked at it, looked at my face, and trudged off towards the sink area. I went to a stall and threw up, trying not to let my legs touch the ground even though the lower left leg of my jeans was already soaked in urine.

Over the past few months, I had had several "is this rock bottom?" moments. Maybe four. Each time it seemed the answer was clearly yes. But I don't think you really ever know if you've hit rock bottom. First you need to determine whether anything that's come before is worse than what's happening right now. That might seem straightforward. But since you think you're near rock bottom, your judgment is at least clouded, if not deeply impaired. You have no context. And even if you feel confident you're there, you know you are now more spectacularly broken and f—ed up than you have ever been in your life, you can't really say you've hit rock bottom. Because that implies it can't get worse. And while you might not be able to imagine things getting worse, that doesn't mean that they won't get worse. So really the job of gauging when you hit your own personal rock bottom should be left for your friends and family when you're gone. At your funeral, after the service over drinks, they are best positioned to sort out the time and place you hit rock bottom. Piecing it together might take some time, depending on who saw what.

I wasn't thinking about this as I used the JFK-flavored handsoap to try to get the urine smell out of my black jeans. I was grateful that the color of my jeans made the stains harder to see. But I knew that however much soap I used, and however wet I allowed my jeans to get, I was going to smell a bit like urine for the next 24 hours of air travel. And somewhere not far from here there was a passenger who was going to bear the burden of proximity to me and my smell. That poor, poor soul.

It would be fair to ask at this point why I passed out in a urinal at JFK airport. And while there isn't one answer, the simplest one is that I thought I needed to be very drunk to go through with what I was doing. I thought that alcohol would help me sort of lose myself. The problem was I didn't have the money to drink at the airport bar, let alone on the plane. I had 65 dollars on me. This was the full extent of my travel money on a one-way trip to Thailand. And for the first time in my adult life, I had no working credit cards.

So my plan was to bring an Evian full of vodka and drink it in the security line, right in that area where bottled waters go to die. So I drank about three shots of vodka during the 10-minute wait. And as I threw away my empty water bottle, I really felt like I'd beaten the system somehow. I was smuggling alcohol past security simply by having just swallowed it.

But as I wander out of the bathroom, still rubbing my wet black jeans, I'm aware of the shortcomings of this plan. And it becomes clear to me that the only way I'm going to get through this is to have a cigarette. Earlier that summer, as my life descended into a haze of alcohol, drugs, and debt I started smoking again. I hadn't smoked since college.

For my sister Jenny there was nothing worse. She didn't try to do anything about the drugs and alcohol until near the end. But when I showed up at a July 4th barbecue, jittery on coke, and slurring from the gin and tonics, she smelled smoke on my clothes and freaked out. She got me on the patch and called me twice every day until I quit, asking me about nothing else, none of the other incredibly harmful and self-hating actions I was engaging in. And I appreciated it. And even as I was breaking every boundary of civility for the rest of that summer and into early fall, I didn't smoke.

But my defenses were gone, and I walked up to the counter of the bookshop/pharmacy/candy store and buy a pack of cigarettes, ignoring the large, printed note my sister stuck inside my wallet begging her to call me before I break down. I'm way past help. I go into the glass-enclosed smoking prison they have constructed in the airport and smoke up with the other weak ones. My entire body convulses with relief. Everything is much better. The breathing you're doing now is deeper and more life-sustaining than what you've been putting yourself through. You believe your body's lies because you cannot argue with how you feel.

I go back to the gate, and I watch the people on stand-by, the sad people at the mercy of the airplane gate travel administrators. There is one woman in particular whose face is ashen. She looks like she could be a friend of my sister. She may, in fact, be a friend of my sister. I feel for her.

But I have my own problems. People are beginning to hover in the area where you are not supposed to line up until your zone has been called. I don't want to check my luggage. When you put everything you have in the world into a piece of carry-on luggage, you want the freedom to at least have it with you. But I couldn't deal with the zone jockeys, so I sit down on the ground, leaning against a large circular column next to a kid playing on an iPad that he had plugged in, ensuring he'd fly with a device as fully juiced as possible. I grasp at my boarding pass in my left jeans pocket. The urine on it is drying. The nicotine hit is wearing off.

I look back at the gate. The woman on stand-by looks so sad. The gate travel administrators are standing back from the desk, apparently with no information available or no willingness to share information right now. There is something in her expression. She is sure she's not going to get on this plane. And it will devastate her. Because someone needs her right now.

An amateur psychologist would say I am running away from my problems. A trained psychologist would probably say it as well. Pretty much anyone who knows the facts of my situation would say it. It's a fact.

So as I start thinking that the brave thing to do, the mature thing, would be to give this person my ticket. She actually seems like she's supposed to be on this plane. And I start thinking about it. This woman needs a boarding pass, I have one.

But in the end, I'm not ready to screw over the guys who bought my ticket. I'd be instantly expanding my realm of failure and cosmic debt to the other side of the world. So I close my eyes and think about the glass-encased house of smoke and whether I could get back and forth for a last smoke before take-off. I find closing my eyes helps a little bit and so I keep them closed. I sleep. When I open my eyes, stand-by woman is nudging me. They are calling my name as they're about to shut the gate. At first I assume that this is of interest to her because if I'm not on the plane then there is a seat for her. But then I see she has her own boarding pass.

She was nudging me to nudge me. I nod in appreciation, and she hurries off to the gate. I watch her hand over her boarding pass. I'm glad she's on the plane. I look back and see the gate numbers and can almost make out the number 22 which is the gate by the smoking house.

"Sir? This gate is about to close." I nod. I turn and squint towards Gate 22. I stand up. I walk straight ahead to the gate and the impatient gate person. "Quickly, sir." I take out my boarding pass, still damp with urine and JFK bathroom water.

I've always judged people in these types of jobs harshly when I see them wearing sanitary gloves, not thinking that one day I will be handing someone a pissed-up boarding pass. The scanner thing doesn't like it and she looks annoyed, and I think I'm really going to have to invent an excuse for how I wet my boarding pass. But it goes through, and she gives it back and I am on my way out of this life and into another one.

I look down the narrow runway and swallow hard. I haven't told anyone I know that I'm doing this. I am burning so many more bridges. No, all the bridges are burned already, really.

The bridges are f—ed. But this will make reconstruction of replacement bridges pretty much impossible. I walk forward. I have to check my bag because there's no room in the compartments. They put a tag on it and say I'll get it back at the runway after the flight. Still, it makes me feel rudderless somehow, not to have anything to drag up the aisle, my belongings now down to my crappy Jansport laptop bag.

Walking down the aisle I feel like passengers blame me, like I've already been holding them up. The plane is full, and my seat is towards the back. From a few rows away I see the only open seat is next to stand-by woman.

I attached a lot of meaning to her getting onto this plane. In that moment I realize I had dreamed about her when I was sleeping, a deeply emotional dream that vanished immediately from my memory but left me feeling like we had been through something together.

I sit down next to her, and she smiles briefly but says

nothing. This is sort of a relief. My curiosity about why she's on this plane is far outweighed by my desire to be left alone. I'm also aware that within 90 minutes or so I will be an itchy, sweaty ball of nerves. She is in the middle seat which is a vulnerable position to be in. It doubles your chances of dealing with a rude, smelly or (overly) talkative person.

When you think about it so many things about modern living discourage physical interactions with real people. We shop online, we socialize on phones, we have our food delivered. We have a network of friends, relatives and business partners who we tolerate seeing in person. But beyond that, the physical presence of strangers is distasteful. They have not been vetted; I have never "Liked" anything of theirs nor have they "Liked" anything of mine. We do not have any mutual Friends. So how can I be expected to sit comfortably next to one of them on these impossibly small chairs, spaced as tightly together as the authorities will allow?

This is my typical mindset towards fellow travellers. But this woman was no longer a stranger to me. I'd spied her during the drama of stand-by, she roused me kindly to help me make my plane and I'd already had a dream about her. She was now among the closest people to me in the world. But I was aware she might not necessarily feel the same about me. Particularly given how I looked, and probably smelled. I was, in my current state, a high-risk seat-mate. So I would need to make an effort to build her trust. This would begin with the greatest gift you can give to a fellow traveller: extended silence.

It's great when people are friendly. I like friendly people and I try to be friendly to others. But for an airline seatmate you really don't want someone who's too friendly. Someone who might not shut up for the duration of this flight. So I will avoid that, I will not speak to her at least until after an hour or so after take-off. There will be time, there is plenty of time. And if I want to know what brought her onto the plane, and I find I do more than I would think, there is no rush to get it out of her.

On the other side of stand-by woman is this very polished, Banana Republic guy with moussed back hair and expensive-looking glasses. Both times I glanced at him he was doing some kind smoothing out of his jacket as if to make sure it wouldn't wrinkle during the trip. I hate him. He takes out his cell phone and starts speaking in an intent whisper to someone about an unsatisfactory decision they made regarding a rented car. I don't hear the details, but it confirms my assumptions about him. As he puts away his cell, the woman takes out a book. I can't see it at first and I don't want to crane my neck to try to make it out. I consider what it could be, what it might be. It could be any manner of genre bestseller, romance, mystery or whatever. And that wouldn't be so bad, really. It's a 17-hour flight and we just want to get away and be somewhere else. It wouldn't be definitive marker of anything. Still, I find myself hoping it's something good, something I can speak to. If I have read the situation correctly this flight could be some kind of turning point for her, as it is for me. So her choice of book might reflect a kind of longing or regret. Names flit around my head: Austen, Checkhov, Woolf, Ishirugo.

Besides the 20 minutes at the gate, I haven't slept in 36 hours. And I am ready to close my eyes, but the plane takes off and as it does so, she turns to look out the window and flashes the cover of her book to me.

Saramago. F—ing Saramago. I've avoided him for some reason. When I was in college someone gave me a Saramago, and I was about to read it and then he won the Nobel Prize and for some reason that ruined it for me. The idea of being seen reading the current Nobel winner. And then when he died, I thought, sh—, I have to read this guy. But then it was the same thing. There was all this Saramago-appreciation stuff and I thought it would feel kind of morbid and cynical to be walking around with one of his books. As if his death made him more important suddenly.

I never got around to it and now it's biting me in the ass. I have nothing to say on Saramago. No small witticism, either respectful or teasing, showing I got the Saramago vibe, that I knew the ride she was on. It would only take one Saramago-appreciating comment to make her feel that we are contemporaries, fellow intellectuals. We were going to be in this together, allies against the airline and its sh—ty rules and sh—ty food, allies against this slick, put-together guy on the window. If I'd just read my Saramago.

Second Place
Impasse
Kenneth Robbins
Ruston, Louisiana

"It all began when Santa's helpers demanded Universal Elf Care."
— J.S. Mason, *The Ghost Therapist...And Other Grand Delights*

ONE

It is 10:30 p.m. mid-September 1978, in an upper-middle-class suburb of Jacksonville, Florida, 1561 Dorado Estates. The house sits at the apex of a cul-de-sac, somewhat removed from the road and its closest neighbors. Its lawn is perfectly manicured, its front walk composed of individual granite slabs, its front door painted deep red to match the red brick of the rest of the house. The principal frontage feature of the home, aside from the two sprawling live oaks that shade the front yard and the even larger white pine to the side, is the large picture window that reveals a living room decorated by a stay-at-home mom: richly textured with faux ritzy fabric, fake crystal, and a rose-patterned wall-paper that could use with a bit of TLC.

Inside the house at 1561 Dorado Estates is one of our leading characters, John Herbert, Superintendent of Schools for Duval County School System. He is a sallow man, small in stature, slightly pudgy but not fat, balding, ambitious. He sits in his Lazy Boy recliner, his feet up, a copy of the city newspaper, the Florida *Times-Union*, resting on his lap as he gives his attention to the local newscast via his color Philco television set, perched on a specially made entertainment table that also holds a Pioneer stereo set with all the components, including a state-of-the-art turntable, two oversized speakers, and a rack of vinyl records neatly tucked inside their jackets. The news on the TV is concerned with the Iranian earthquake which, according to early reports, is supposed to have killed over twenty-five thousand people. Aftershocks, says the reporter, continue to shatter homes and destroy lives. Herbert is only passively interested in what he is being told through still photos of what appears to be massive destruction and human tragedy.

Sheila Herbert approaches her husband from the recently renovated kitchen with two mugs of coffee, decaffeinated. She is a former high school beauty queen, still attractive in spite of being one year beyond thirty, but, with her hair in a ponytail and her face smeared with a green exfoliating cream, it is difficult to see exactly what she once might have been though in her head still is. She is dressed for bed, a loose-fitting t-shirt with the words "Ponte Vedra Beach" stencilled on the front, a pair of her husband's bright blue boxer shorts, and slippers which slide loosely on the carpeted floor, indicating the kind of hectic day she is bringing to a close. She gives one of the mugs to Herbert who sips it gingerly, sensitive to its heat. She slips casually onto the welcoming sofa that sits with its back to the plate glass window. She sighs, pulls her legs under her in a way that makes her tendency to strike alluring poses seem habitual, and says, "Horrible, isn't it."

"What?"

"So much death and destruction. In Iran. Whole villages destroyed." She nods toward the TV, controlling her desire to change channels. After all, *Columbo,* her favorite television series, is re-airing its final segment this very night. She had missed the original screening of the episode due to a PTA meeting, one she was prohibited from missing, her being the wife of the Superintendent. It is her anticipation for the final episode that had made her day worth enduring. Secretly, she harbors a crush on the show's star, Peter Falk; it is his glass eye that makes him so alluring.

Herbert grunts. "Wasn't paying any attention."

She can't change TV stations, though she really wants to. After all, it was her husband who had first turned it on, and the unwritten law of the house is that the television belongs to he or she who first claims it. So, she tries another tactic, "You did well tonight, John. Were you nervous?"

He grunts again. "Why should I be? Nothing to be nervous about." He doffs the mug of coffee in her direction, "Good. Thanks." His eyes focus, not on the news report from Tabas, Iran, which is now in transition to the local weather, but on his wife who has gotten quite comfortable on the sofa. He says, barely above a whisper, "Don't sit there, honey."

"Why not? May I switch channels?"

"Seriously," he says with more verve. "Don't sit there. Please."

She changes channels without permission. She would run naked through the streets if Peter Falk asked her to. She has to rise from her sofa to accomplish this little task, so now, she stands in his way. "Where do you want me to sit?"

"Away from the window."

She sits on the floor at his feet, placing her arm across his thighs, rubbing her braless breasts against his knee. "Is this better?"

He is now reading the newspaper. "Much."

"I don't understand," she says, using her pouty tone-of-voice.

"Then, turn the TV off."

"No, I mean. . ." She shifts her position so she can look him directly in his face. She doesn't know what she expects to see. "The window. Is there something wrong with it?"

"Of course not, don't be silly. Could be somebody out there for all we know. Looking in. Some weird people in this town."

It isn't like her to press, it isn't her style, but then, she has never before been chastened for sitting on her own sofa. "How long have we lived in this house, sweetie?"

"Long enough. Wanna move?"

"No!" How dare he, she wants to know but fears to ask, pose such an important question in such a casual way. Yes, she wants to move, but now is not the time for such a consuming question. "So, why would some weirdo be looking at us through our window on this particular night? You're acting strange." She thinks she knows the answer to such a question as she straightens her shoulders, creating a perfectly manicured pose on the floor at his feet.

He squirms a bit. "Headache. Watch your program."

She rises, moves behind him. "Let me rub your temples for you. You've been under such pressure all summer long. All this labor union brouhaha."

He pushes her aside. "Not that kind of headache."

She is eying the comfort of the sofa as she says, "You're working too hard."

"It's not that."

"What then?"

His irritation is growing. "Look, if you're not going to watch TV, then turn it off and go to bed."

She seats herself in the overstuffed chair near the front entry. "I liked you better before. This job of yours. . ."

He snaps: "Pays the bills! I have a lot on my mind, that's

all."

"I thought you solved all your problems with tonight's debate. You have a family, you know, not just a job." She waits for his next retort, but he has decided to ignore her, something that has gotten easier for him to do of late. "Well?" she persists.

He shrugs. "Watch TV."

She is up again, making a move toward the sofa. "This isn't as comfortable as the couch."

"Stay away from the sofa I said!"

She is becoming as irritable as he as she says, "You're being unreasonable."

He slams the newspaper to the floor. "Are we gonna fight over the goddamn furniture?"

She bristles. "Whoa there, Mr. John Herbert, you don't have to talk that way to me. Save that kind of language for your friends at the Union. What if Bobby had been here for that silly outburst?"

"I wouldn't have said it if Bobby had been here."

"Oh, so it's all right to curse me? First, I can't sit on my own fully-paid-for and comfortable sofa, thank you very much, and now you curse me?"

"I'm not in the mood, hon."

"I'm not one of your teachers, you know. You may talk that way to them, but in this house. . ."

His anger is becoming too intense, so he feels the need to cool himself with a sip of hot coffee. "I'll turn the TV off. Okay?"

She is ready to explode. "Why won't you let me sit on my own sofa!"

"Because—"

But he does not complete his thought. It is interrupted by

glass flying from the window into the center of the sitting room followed almost immediately by the sound of a 12-gauge shotgun expending both barrels simultaneously. A fragment of glass nicks Sheila's right forehead above her eyebrow causing a burst of blood to drip onto her precious t-shirt and to the floor. She drops her coffee mug and the liquid splatters across the room to be absorbed by the cream-colored carpet as an irreparable stain. She follows her mug to the floor, clasping her bleeding forehead as her blood mixes with the green of her facial treatment, creating a flow that is repulsive to see.

It is as if time has become cold molasses trying to be poured from its bottle. Things are enhanced, slowed to a point that she can actually hear the car outside the window ignite, backfire, and drive away speedily into the night. The noise from the TV is equally slowed so that she can feel the words being spoken with her nose and mouth. The words coming from her husband are equally unsavory: "Sheila! Sheila, are you . . .? Don't move. Stay where you are!"

The next words she hears send shivers throughout her frightened body. "Mommy? What happened?"

It is her son, Bobby, aged eight-and-a-half who stands in the hall archway, dressed in his special Mickey Mouse Club pajamas. "Bobby!" she screeches as she rushes to hold him tight.

"Mommy, you're bleeding."

"Oh, Bobby, Bobby, my baby!"

John Herbert is at the window, looking out, then on the telephone, then hanging up, then staring at the buckshot blast that has redecorated the mantel above the useless fireplace which now, somehow or other, possesses his brain: Why a fireplace in Jacksonville, Florida, in September, in this heat, and why hadn't he had a fireplace in the home he once owned in

Duluth, Minnesota. It makes no sense. None of it makes any sense anymore. At least the blast has spared the Pioneer entertainment center.

He stands, awed, perplexed, and a trifle angry as he whispers for no one to hear, "I told you to stay away from the window...."

The TV weather forecaster continues: "Partly cloudy tomorrow with scattered afternoon showers. And no relief from this heat wave, I'm sorry to say."

TWO

Let's back up a bit, okay? Late January.

Meet Frasier Pardue, known to his close friends, what few he has, as Frilly. How Frilly is devised from Frasier is a puzzlement. Doctor Pardue is three years beyond the normal retirement age when he enters the office of John Herbert, his Assistant Superintendent of Schools. He is the sort of man who commands attention as he takes up more space than is usually considered healthy. His girth is enhanced by his lack of height: meaning, he is obese beyond comfortable obesity. Perhaps that is what has led him to confront his younger associate on this early Friday morning and caused him to sit with his right foot resting comfortably on the cushioned seat of another chair.

"Got a minute?" he asks Herbert. "Course you do. You got nothing but minutes, I know how it is. I got something for you that you just might like."

"What's happening, Frilly?"

"Just wanted you to be the first to know." A sigh comes from inside the expansive chest as if something is trying to escape what surely has been part of a long and torturous journey. "First to know. Come July 1st, I'm quitting, John. Simple as that.

Retirement, they say, has its perks."

"Shoot. Get outta here. You? You can't quit." But Herbert knows this is not the truth. He has been waiting for the old fool to step aside for the past three years. In fact, he had taken the assistant superintendent position because of Doctor Pardue's accelerating age and waning health.

It's about time, he wants to bellow. But doesn't. Instead, he quips, "You and retirement will never be friends."

"I'll be meeting with Harriet at two to turn in my formal document. If that's okay by you." Harriet is everybody's boss; we'll be meeting her later.

"Hell, Doctor Pardue," Herbert protests, "you've got years left, you know that."

"Yeah. Years. If I'm lucky. Years to do a few of the things I've wanted to do my entire life." He leans forward. "You got any idea what doing my job for the past twenty-eight years has cost me?"

"I could make a guess or two."

"Plenty, my son, plenty. Anyway," the older and larger educator says with a smirk on his face, "I always said that I'd know when it was time. And with the issues we're all facing, with the DTU raising all sorts of noise, the time couldn't be better."

"So. Why are you telling me this?"

"I'm telling Harriet that the Board needs you to step up, to take my place. You know the landscape. You know where the mines are buried. You can keep this damn system afloat. And she needs to know that you have my recommendation."

"I ask again. Why are you telling *me* all of this?"

It is easy to see the years taking a toll on the retiring superintendent. Just watch his eyes twist this way and that, not seeing, not looking, only darting like bats at twilight. "I need to know if you want this effing job. Before I make any recommendation, if you want to replace me?"

Herbert is the model for "cool." He laces his fingers behind his head as he rocks in his comfortable desk chair. "Do or don't is irrelevant. The Board will undertake a national search. You know that."

"But I don't know if you'll put your name in the pot. Will you?"

"It's worth considering." He is rising, looking for a reason to end this less than fruitful interview. He has more pressing things to be doing.

"If you do, I can assure you," Frasier Pardue says with his eyes cast to the well-worn space rug that covers much of the floor, "the job is yours."

"Hmmm," Herbert says, more a sigh than an actual utterance. "I'd do things differently, you know. I may not follow you the way you might want."

"All I want from you is this." His eyes are focused now on the face of the man who is bound to be his successor. "One thing and one thing only. *Kill* the goddamn union. And *bury* it. Whatever it takes. Just. Kill it."

"Whatever it takes?"

"Whatever."

"If I am chosen—if it is offered—if I accept it. . . It will be my pleasure."

So. Our story has begun.

TWO POINT FIVE

Truth be told, Doctor Frasier Pardue didn't retire. No. He didn't last that long.

On Valentine's Day, while walking his Scottish terrier, named Barry after his favorite politician of all time, one Mr. Goldwater, the superintendent feels a surge of anxiety form behind his left lung and a sharp slicing pain blasting through his left shoulder into his elbow and wrist. At first he thinks it is simple angina, something that has plagued him off and on for the past decade. Only this time it is different. It is too intense. The panic button located somewhere behind his left ear is already in action, causing him to turn abruptly toward his front yard. Only he doesn't make it. He collapses on the edge of the sidewalk, his short, stubby legs poking across the curb and into the street. No sooner has his head found the strip of grass between sidewalk and curb, he draws his final breath. He lets go of Barry's leash. He lets go of his sense of self. He lets go of his hold on life. Barry barks as loudly as he can and tugs mightily at his master's trouser leg, but to no avail. It takes a neighbor, disgusted by the racket the dog is making, several minutes before she seeks and then finds the cause. After calling 911, she takes Barry home with her, hoping to get the mutt to shut up.

Dr. Pardue's demise makes the front page of the local newspaper. He was either adored or abhorred, both for the same fundamental reason: how he had done his job. Now it is up to the Board to find his replacement. The day after his funeral, the national search begins. And John Herbert waits until the final week of the announced search before putting in his application: he didn't want to appear too eager. He doesn't. Once his application is received, Harriet Sniderman, Chairwoman of the Board, breaths freely for the first time since

Valentine's Day. Maybe her school system can be kept more or less intact after all.

Third Place
May Oak Murders
Lydia Malone
Tallahassee, Florida

It took four men and a manual forklift to move the rusted cast iron stove from its nook, nestled in a foot of pine needles and dried magnolia leaves that had blown under the carriage house roof. Despite its age and the decades of neglect, its stalwart construction proved the iron beast worthy of one last fight. The men maneuvered the stove back and forth, scraping the feet of the ornately molded legs over deteriorating bricks. Their foreheads and forearms were already shining, slick with sweat.

The clay from these red hills was terrible for brickmaking. Old pavers like this were often of the clinker brick variety: uneven in coloring, tink-tink-clink sounding when plopped together in a mortar row. So many of the old houses downtown had misshapen cisterns and wobbly driveways fashioned from the knobbly masonry.

Clementine secretly loved the sound of the old bricks, despite how expensive they were to replace during restorations. Paying old whiskered masons to hand pack the clay and fire them in their beehive kilns was always a decent line item in the budget. But that was a project for next year's grant cycle, she figured. This summer was all about the inventory. Mr. Coturn was finally dead.

***

The old stove used to be the workhorse of the kitchen, a room built as far away from the other activities of the house as possible to keep the heat, smells, and clamor out of the posh parlors and the elder Coturn's home study. The sounds of sizzling onions or frying potatoes weren't meant for the ears of the delicate class. At least, that was the argument when the kitchen was added on at the turn of the century. Before, the cookery was set further back on the property, cleaving a visible separation between the well-to-do occupants of the home and the hired help scrubbing away at the pots and pans of breakfast, lunch, and supper. At that time, it was more improper to mix company than to let the smell of a delicious roast permeate throughout the hallways.

A small pine placard was affixed beside the front door, its inlay painted black to make the raised characters easier to read from afar: "Radner-Coturn House, Est. Ca. 1842." This house had seen a lot of history roam through its doorways, parade past its porch, and unfold like the springtime flowers in the chain of parks across the street.

All of these snippets of ethnography flitted through Clementine's mind as she stepped further back, giving the men and the forklift plenty of space to ease the old iron beast from its carriage house cave. As ginger as they were with palms slipping from sweat and a slurry of rust, bits of the stove creaked and wobbled in protest. The cover to a hot plate shifted and tilted in its corresponding hole, misshapen from years of moving on and off to make room for a pot or a frying pan. The man nearest the tilted plate tried to flip it back into place and found the task harder than anticipated. The plate was doing its best impression of the Titanic, slanted at an angle that had wedged it more into the incorrect alignment as the rest of the movers tugged and rolled the stove over the bumpy bricks.

"Hey, will y'all stop a minute so I get this piece to fit back in?" he asked his crew. The stove stopped moving, only slightly teetering on an even section of the courtyard.

The plate was perched just above the stove's firebox, the hottest section for cooking back when it was in service. That meant there was a convenient door to the section underneath the plate, which the mover (Clementine thought his name might be Randall, but she wasn't sure) took as a fortuitous sign. He hooked a finger onto the little door and tugged gently, testing the hinges and the years of rusted gunk around the seal. His first try unsuccessful, he pulled with a touch more force the second time. The door let out a small squeak of metal-on-metal objection, swinging open on unhappy hinges. Clementine imagined that the interior was grimy with soot and humidified carbon.

Randall ducked down to peer in, seeing only a dark box in shadow in the late afternoon sunlight. He carefully stuck his hand into the firebox, feeling for the tilted plate along the top of the short shaft. Not even three inches in, he felt the plate and tried to shift it back into a horizontal position.

"Ooh!" Randall snatched his hand back, the plate clanging back into its slightly inset position. "There must be an old log in there still. The back of my hand touched it. It was…crusty."

He didn't look pleased, but he also was used to handling dirty antiques left to rot in the elements in various ways in backyards, junk piles, and amateur antique hoarders' poorly insulated warehouses. He reached into his back pocket to retrieve his cellphone, touching the screen twice to turn the flashlight function on. Shining the little beam into the firebox, he bent over to give the inside a good look.

"Might be a nest of something, too, so it's not a bad idea to check for critters before we move 'er to the warehouse," another crew member, John, offered. Randall nodded. Clementine agreed, not wanting to have to pull out another family of cats from an artifact as she'd had to do a few years ago on another restoration project. That had been a little traumatic.

"I think it's an old log, honestly. Just poorly mummified by the Florida heat," Randall said. He reached back in to see how deteriorated the log might be. "It'd be easier to just brush it out here rather than have it get all over the back of the truck."

But when he went to dislodge the log from the firebox, it didn't really budge the right way. Clementine could tell from Randall's face that whatever the texture was that he encountered with a fuller grip was not what he was expecting. He stopped abruptly, pulling his hand back out again. He looked at his fingers, which were covered in something: a mixture of rust, grime, and now some sort of disintegrating fiber. John looked at his hands as well, a frown of disgust forming on his face.

"I don't think it's a log. I think it might be a dead animal, honestly. A really dead animal. Maybe a possum crawled in there one night and died." His face mirrored John's, nose scrunched up like a pug's. "Does anyone have an old plastic bag they'd like to donate to the cause?"

Randall looked up and around for a willing volunteer.

"I got you," Clementine piped up, trotting off to her little hatchback parked just outside the back gate. She knew she had plenty of random bags from the quick gas station stops she made for snacks between project sites and research rooms. She pulled a yellow dollar store bag from the back seat, the rumpled "Thank You" a cheery reminder of the chocolate bar it no doubt ferried from the cash register to her car.

She returned, handing the bag to Randall to use like a doggy bag for rover's leftovers. He turned the bag inside out over his hand, reaching into the firebox with more confidence now that whatever was in there wouldn't make direct contact with his palm. For a few moments, the crew stood by, living vicariously through Randall's facial expression journey. By Clementine's measure, it looked squishier than anticipated with a side of "ew."

"Got it," he said, pulling everything out and setting the bag on top of the stove. John still had his hands bracing the stove, the backsplash and warming oven on top very easily made unstable on the forklift tines. He peered at the lump with suspicion.

Randall opened the bag back up once again, trying to make out what the stove had hidden from sight before. "I honestly can't tell what it is," he said, rolling the plastic down, "since it's so wrinkled. But where's the head?" he mused, as everyone tried to fit the shape to a mental image of a possum, cat, or even a large squirrel.

"I don't think it's a critter after all. Unless it was a snake?"

A pause.

"Is that bone?" John pointed at the end closer to his side of the stove.

"Uh… maybe? I'm not touching it again to find out."

John leaned over. He squinted. His frown deepened. "It might be a deer leg, honestly. Mr. Coturn was a hunter, after all. Could have had something to do with it."

"Well, just make sure there's nothing else in there before we finish moving this thing. If it's venison jerky, it's past its prime for sure," the third mover suggested. Kyle might have been his name, although that morning's introductions were so long ago in Clementine's mind. They'd already lugged out a series of mule-drawn hunting carts, a couple banged up car bumpers, and a derelict monitor-top refrigerator from the 1920s. Mr. Coturn, forever the bachelor, had never really disposed of anything he thought he could fix up and use again. He got that frugality from his mother, a collector of antiques and a pincher of pennies.

Clementine, without missing a beat, handed Randall another plastic bag. "I figured it could be a multiple bag affair," she said, grinning.

Randall chuckled. "Everything old Coturn was involved with was a multiple this or that affair, from what I can tell." Everyone laughed.

He reached in once again and carefully raked along the bottom of the firebox for any lingering bits of what they now believed was ancient deer meat. As before, he set the bag and its contents atop of the stove. He peeped into the bag for the next collection of unidentified bits.

This time, he looked even more perturbed at what he'd fished out. John and Kyle also lost their smiles from laughing a moment before.

"I don't think that's a deer leg after all." John shuddered.

Not unless the deer Coturn hunted had evolved to have fingers.

***

Despite the small street grid of the town's layout, rush hour was rush hour, and it took Doc Macrae about a half-hour to get from the police station to the old mansion downtown.

Swinging a bowed leg from the cab of an old pick-up truck, he looked like he was ready to step out of an old spaghetti western flick at most public appearances. No one was exactly sure if it was an intentional fashion choice, or if the phrase "intentional fashion choice" had ever crossed his mind. Most folks just let him do his work in his cowboy regalia in peace, because he was, after all, the most senior detective at the station.

The heels of his boots clinked against the brick pathway leading from the park-side road down to the back of the property, to the courtyard where the moving crew and Clementine stood waiting. Clementine had called the non-emergency line of the police department, trying to describe the unexpected finding of a dismembered arm without sounding culpable. She stood just outside the gate to wave the detective down and around the mansion's back staircase to the area they were clearing. She'd never met him before, but he matched the description Kyle had given her when he wondered aloud who they'd send to investigate the bags of forgotten forearm.

"Doc Macrae knew Mr. Coturn from way back when, so they might send him out, if he's not busy," Kyle mused. "He knows this house better than some of Mr. Coturn's extended family. He used to hunt with the old guy back when he was a kid."

Armed with that knowledge, Clementine attempted to place Doc Macrae in some sort of generation. Was he her parents' age? Her grandmother's? How old was Mr. Coturn when he died, anyway? The Coturns had been in this old house since the 1920s, in the city since the turn of the century. They hadn't helped found the town or anything as genealogically or geographically noble as that, but they were prominent enough, given that the elder Coturn was a statesman. The more recently late Mr. Coturn was more of a playboy, a lifelong bachelor who owned horses, fast cars, and many smart pinstripe suits. Still, he had been soft-spoken and respectful the handful of times Clementine had been able to meet with him to create his home's historic preservation plan. Mr. Coturn's estate planner was a little more curt with her.

"Ms. Pennock?" Doc Macrae inquired, a hand extended in an absent-minded introduction. "Where's the arm? Around here?"

"Yes," she said, only giving his palm a fleeting squeeze before he rounded the corner and made his way to the old cast iron stove. The moving crew was getting antsy: it was nearly six in the evening, and their contracted work hours were technically up at five. However, they didn't want to unload the stove only to reload it the next day.

"Boys, you will have to leave the stove here. I'll need to poke around a bit more, and it technically is evidence in whatever this is." Doc Macrae gestured at the half empty carriage house stalls, some still packed with old bits of furniture and equipment, others blanketed in a few years' worth of decomposing yard detritus. "If you need to unload it off your forklift, go ahead."

Randall coughed. John shook his head. None of them wanted to move the stove again, even if the forklift was company property. "We can prop it up so it's stable for you. Lock the wheels. It's heavy enough it won't roll away, it's just top-heavy," John said.

The men spent a few minutes building a rough buttress out of some two-by-fours they found stacked under the back stairs. The uneven surface of the bricks was an advantage, as they allowed them to wedge the wood just so and give the old stove a back brace.

"Call us when you're ready to complete the move, Ms. Clementine," Kyle said, as the men shuffled out of the courtyard toward their work trucks. Clementine felt since she was the project manager, she had to be the one to stay with the detective while he did his preliminary survey.

He looked at her, expecting her to leave with the workmen. She decided he was only a little younger than her grandmother, and about twice as judgmental.

"My contract stipulates my guardianship of the property and its artifacts for the duration of this grant cycle, so I have to stay with you," she offered as professionally as she could.

He nodded slightly. If he'd been wearing a proper ten-gallon hat, she could easily imagine an "Arighty, ma'am," from him. She was spared, however.

"So y'all found this in pieces?" he asked her, using a pen to steadfastly rifle through the bag with the fingers.

"Yes, Randall only pulled the bigger... chunks out first. He thought it was a possum who crawled in there and died."

Doc Macrae let a small smirk deepen the wrinkles around his mouth. He was clean-shaven, but his eyebrows bushed out to punctuate his expressions for him. The eyebrows were decidedly grandfatherly to Clementine.

"Normally, I'd agree with him. Happens all the time. People find them in their chimneys or dryer ducts. You can usually smell them before you find them."

Clementine nodded, saying, "Yeah, the guys were saying that as well. I guess it's more common than I've experienced. But I rent, so I don't have a fireplace to capture unsuspecting marsupials."

He nodded again, now shining a small but proper flashlight into the firebox that had been the arm's housing for however long.

"Did y'all open any of the other oven doors?"

"No, I didn't even think to do so." That was true. She'd been more concerned with the one limb than with looking for any more accompanying parts. She wasn't as freaked out about discovering a hunk of human being as one might think; then again, she'd worked as an archaeological consultant on projects that turned up bits and bones a few times. What was scarier to her was stopping movement on the grant project in order to adhere to the federal law of Section 106. The next grant payout was a month away, and boy, did her checking account look forward to that deposit raising the balance like a buoy at high tide.

Doc Macrae deftly pulled at the next lower door, where the ash from the firebox would gather back when the stove was in regular use. It probably had a muddy paste of soot and coals, if not a sticky residue from neglect and pest droppings. The detective aimed his flashlight's beam into the larger cavity, revealing a patina of carbon but, thankfully, no other body parts.

He proceeded to repeat the process on the main oven door and the warming oven up top.

The stove's pipe was back in the storage area, half hidden by leaves and dilapidation. It was vaguely crumpled, as if something heavy (like a cast iron stove) had accidentally fallen atop it and squashed it into its misshapen form. Still, Doc Macrae made his way over to the pipe to give it the same investigative treatment. Satisfied with a lack of remnants in the pipe, he returned to Clementine and the stove.

"So I'll need you to come back with me to the station," he said as he began jotting down a few spidery bullet points in a pocket notepad. Clementine blinked, finally truly surprised by an event today. "To make the formal statement about this southpaw we've got here. It shouldn't take too long. I know you didn't put this souvenir here."

Young Adult Novel Excerpt
Final Judge — Joyce Sweeney
Coral Springs, Florida

First Place
Atlantis' Son
Katie Clark
Tallahassee, Florida

Chapter One

Uriel often gazed at the stars at night and wondered where his homeworld lay, many, many galaxies away. The star masters would know, but he was no star master. Tonight, he stood on a rock overlooking the sea. He had run away from the tedious meeting with the guild masters. As a councilman's son, it was his responsibility to learn statecraft, to entertain and balance the emotions of the many factions. He knew this, yet, if he had to listen to one more farm master give his tally of sheep, or the tapestry master complain about the lack of said sheep's wool, his head would implode. Worse, he feared that he would make one of the guild person's head explode as he had not yet gained total control of his gift.

Not that he was exactly hiding. Anyone who knew him could find him, and there was no hiding from his father. Through the gift, he always knew the location of his son.

Uriel let out a sigh, picked up a rock, and threw it across the crashing waves. "Kerplunk." The resulting ripples undulated outwards, echoing the glowing orb of the moon.

"Moon, moon, moon…. What a small name for such a large part of this world," he said to himself. He had been told that the long-lost home world had no such astronomical entity.

"To whom are you speaking, mel Don?" a slender man in a red tunic said.

Startled by the intrusion, he nearly slipped on the algae. "By the stone, you nearly made me tumble into the ocean, Snider! I was speaking to myself. Who else would I be speaking to amongst the waves and stars?"

"My apologies, mel Don; for a minute I thought you were conversing with one of the mer people."

"I wouldn't ever! How could you even think thus?" Uriel stated.

Snider merely shrugged.

"Snider, I know that you were sent by Father to fetch me. I just can't go back to that hall full of squabbling fools just yet. I felt the burn come to me, and I had to get away before I hurt someone," Uriel kicked more rocks over the cliff's edge as if they were the offending voices.

"mel Don, I am only to deliver this message: You must return by quaking hour and be prepared for extra meditation lessons on the morrow," he delivered his message with palms up, then pivoted to leave.

"Wait!" Uriel reached out to Snider's shoulder. "Lately, I just can't stop thinking about Home. You are one of Father's most knowledgeable servants. Could you show me where it is?"

Turning back around, Snider replied, "No, even though I am of the Blood, albeit a small portion, it is not for me to know the secrets of Home. I can never go there. You are better off asking the Learning Master." He grimaced and briskly retreated, his eyes briefly capturing the moon's mournful reflection on the sea.

Pondering the Blood issue, Uriel plopped down on the grass

full of shadows and dew. The soft breeze played with his scarlet locks. He wondered if he would ever be able to control his gift or become like the Deformed: the ones who are controlled by their gift. Picking up a Yreth flower, his worry manifested into picking it apart, blue petal by blue petal. Again, his eyes lifted to the heavens, and he wondered about Home. Although no one had been there in nearly a millennium, it was still revered, especially in the households of the Blood. He remembered stories his Nana told him about pure skies of green, of crystal houses and amethyst seas. Of a people geared toward perfection, yet used their world to their detriment. Lately, this mythical Home pervaded his thoughts, his dreams, his desires.

A shooting star chased the constellations across the sky. The Lamb and Queen; the mermaid and Unitar, all in their nightly dance.

Where in the cosmos was his origin? Why did they have to leave? These questions he had asked, but was told that answers were not his quite yet. As a councilman's son, and one of the Blood, the gift of this knowledge would come upon his man-making.

Sighing, he stood and threw the bare stem of the Yreth to the ground and turned toward the city gate, stretching out his lanky form and nearly stumbling over himself.

Towering above the island, the walls of the capital city gleamed silver in the moonlight. Stout and impenetrable, their crafting now as mysterious as the Blood's origin. It seamlessly encased the capital city, warding out all who wished it harm, and preventing the escape of those ill-favored. At the crest of the hill, and directly on the path Uriel walked, stood a gate of solid crystal. The gates stood open, welcoming all to the faire city, until the hour of the Quake, at which time the gatekeepers closed it fast. Framing the gates stood two massive trees, which were gifts from this world's people upon the landing and creation of the island. Most of the aboriginals regarded the Blood as Gods. Some called them, "Fair folk," referring to their bright copper skin.

Standing next to the trees, in their arson finest, were the gatekeepers.

"Hail, Uriel!" Lost in his revelry, Uriel didn't see the short statured youth to the left of the East gatekeeper. Startled, he stopped his trek and looked for the sound of this interruption.

"Oh, Fallon, I didn't see you," Uriel replied and walked toward Fallon. "What are you doing outside the gates at this hour?"

"I could ask the same of you. It's nearly time for the gates to be shuttered. I am now Asleen's apprentice." He nodded to the East Gate Guard.

Asleen interrupted, "As such, you're not yet finished with your duties. Sorry, mel Don, but you must continue your conversation later."

Frowning, Fallon pivoted and ran toward the gatehouse.

"Meet me at the hall later, Fallon!" Uriel yelled after him.

"Pardon, me, mel Don, but your father instructed me to tell you to meet him at the Temple square in a crow's time." Asleen shifted his spear to his other hand.

Uriel crossed the gate in haste, as he did not wish to be caught outside after the Quake hour. Superstitious though it may be, the Blood believed that certain misfortune would come to those caught outside the protective walls. Many of the Blood who travelled away from the Isle had not returned. And those that had were changed.

He continued down the path, passing the trade shops of the

outer city, staying on the Way to the imposing structure at the crest of the hill–the city's center. Calling the massive temple a building was misleading, as it wasn't completely enclosed, and didn't have a roof.

As he walked up the path, the few tradesmen that remained at the market turned their head in reverence to the Councilman son. Oblivious to this deference, he passed them by. Neither acknowledging their presence, nor outright ignoring them. Nor did he notice the few outright glares given toward his passing, or the small light-skinned children running from stall to stall.

He only saw the bustle that was Circadin, the capital city of Atlantis. Onward, he cantered toward the center, carefully stepping in his lamb-skinned boots so that he wouldn't trip over his overly long legs. The market gave way to the tradesmen's abodes, simple, yet serviceable. Brightly tiled roofs reached two to three stories above the Way. Windowed faces greeted all that passed. At this hour, there were not many outside their houses. If he chose to look, Uriel would have seen the tradesmen and their families gathered around their gate-front alter to prepare for the Quake Hour traditional silence. The oldest youth of each family prepared to light the asreath candle at the signal, and the elder posed to offer their blood sacrifice.

Uriel did notice, however, the slightly salty taste that pervaded this city life and the smell of broiled seafood. The sea had become the city's lifeblood and livelihood. Even though the islanders kept herds of cattle and sheep and traded them in the market, he would rather eat crab than sheep any day.

Uriel started to sweat with the exertion of trekking up the steep Way. He knew that time dwindled, and he needed to find a public sundering stone soon. At last, the terracotta houses gave way to open green space with a long stone standing in the

2022 Seven Hills Review

center of a circle of trees. The stone was dark black and had grooves that led to the ground.

A long, solemn bell tolled, reverberating off the high walls of the temple and buildings. Removing a small knife, Uriel knelt before the stone, and said, "Ancestors of the Blood, we remember. Alta Maray parketa. We remember the land of our birth. We remember the strife that led to the destruction. At this hour of the mighty Quake, we honor your sacrifice with this blood."

Uriel pricked his finger, watching the red-gold liquid well up. Squeezing his finger, he let it drop onto the table. With the contact, the blood smoked and rolled down the engraved sides unto the brazen ground. For a long moment, silence reigned. Even the sea gulls seemed to hold their breath. Suddenly, his arm started to tingle, and his vision blurred. He cried out in dismay and leaned over to steady himself. He felt the same queer feeling he had felt after getting angry at the tradesman's meeting this morning. The world shimmered and he stood outside himself. When the blood hit the ground, his eyes glossed over.

***

The silence was pervasive as if the world held its breath. Not a leaf rustled in the trees, the birds held their song, and even the insects forgot their voice. He looked from his terracotta balcony and could feel the pensive silence.

Then, in the distance, a howl, a mournful cry from one of the many strays of the city. Then, another joined its voice, and another closer to the villa. Oscows, the large black birds of the continent, screeched and took flight. Then the rumbling started. The ground rippled like a pond with a Giant playing with skipping stones. He jumped back into the house, grabbling onto the doorway.

As he did, the balcony collapsed onto the street. His screams and others joined the cacophony of destruction....

***

Uriel awoke screaming, with sweat and tears rolling down his face. His finger, still pounding with the pain of the blood gift, brought him to the Now. The ground no longer shook, the stone still standing stout. He looked around and wondered if any had heard or seen the visage that pervaded his mind.

As he stood, he heard footsteps coming from down the hill. Two tall men in officer's uniforms approached him.

"Hail, mel Don!" the first one yelled. "We heard a cry and feared the worst."

Brushing of the dust, Uriel replied, "Na, it was only a fright. I am ok."

"It's good that you are unhurt. Your father would not be pleased if anything should befall you." The guard leaned his spear against one of the circling trees. "Would you like an escort to the temple?"

"Neah. I am going on my own time," he said.

"In that case, we will go down to the lower guard house and give relief to the day crew."

"Anon, travel safe and be sure footed."

"You as well." Both soldiers bowed their head and ventured down through the lower city. Uriel lingered a minute more, watching their retreat. He felt a gentle breeze on his exposed shoulders and watched the swaying lembass grass and bright pink areal flowers. The lower city lit up from the numerous crystalline lights that captured the Sol's light by day and reflected it by night. By comparison, the inner courtyard was dark and forbidden.

He turned away from the city lights and dark stone. As he continued his trek up the Way and hill, he pondered what he had seen during his Quake hour sacrifice. Had he slipped and somehow hit his head on the stone? He shook his head at the thought. Somehow, the place of his vision seemed familiar. It was as if he had been there many times before, yet he knew that he had not. At least he hadn't been there in any of his 30 Sol rotations.

Small starleene lanterns lined the Way, casting their shadows upon the trees and manicured gardens of the inner courtyard. His legs began to ache from the strain of such an arduous task in a short time. Normally, he would stroll through the gardens and relish the beauty around him. Not tonight. Tonight, the dinner, the stars, the vision all weighed upon him, making his journey that much harder. It was as if his heart pulled him back to the startling cliffs from which he had fled. And he dreaded the meeting with his father, of which he had been at odds of late. He wished that he could speak with his mother, who could always calm his father's smoldering temper.

At last, he came to the outer temple dwellings, where the acolytes kept house. They were simple compared to the terracotta houses of the lower buildings, yet the simplicity reflected an understated elegance. Roads and paths branched out from the way, the largest of these being Temple Way, which went the entire circumference of the city.

Especially at this time of the evening, after the hour of the Quake, a steady stream of people dressed in lightly colored robes quickly rushed from the sacrificial places. They carried pallets of small knives and wheeled wagons full of dead lambs and chickens, now destined for the bakers and of the lower village.

"Excuse me," a young lady in full priestess dress said as she rushed past him on her way to the temple.

The temple was easily the tallest structure in the city. Rising prominently from the ground, its outer walls mirrored those of the city. Seamless, the five walls stood together, yet never touching. The sides were rectangular up to three stories, then tapered to a point. A slender crystalline beam connected all five walls to the top tower.

Most people were awed by this architectural masterpiece. Uriel was not; its splendor had ceased to hold any type of mystery.

Uriel stepped between the walls into the temple square. He knew that his father would be at their family's Rock along the ring of alcoves of the sanctum. Like every other resident of the city, they had an altar in their residence, but the elders of the Blood held their Quake hour ceremony at the temple whenever feasible.

The sweet smell of roasting quail and rosemary wafted down from the temple kitchens and mixed with the metallic smell of blood that pervaded the outer sanctum. The people of the Blood were forbidden to use lesser animals as sacrifice; only their own blood was adequate. From an early age, Uriel was taught the delicate art of drawing blood from his own fingers, and on which days to use which fingers. He had heard horror stories about those who had not followed the rite as instructed. They gave all their blood.

Conversely, it was anathema for anyone not of the Blood to give their own blood. Small folk used animal blood, usually of the small birds and fowl of the island. The more well-off tradesmen and priest were able to afford young lambs or bulls. Afterward, the freshly slaughtered were shipped off to the meat houses.

Outside of the temple kneeled a stout, deeply bronzed pillar of a man. Ridges lined his face and hands, and peppered copper hair. Dark wohl tattoos circled his face and shaved head.

Uriel slowly crept closer to the kneeling elder, careful to make not a sound. With his forefingers, he worried the half-moon amulet that dangled from his neck. The crystalline lanterns cast dancing shadows that seemed to mock Uriel's trepidation.

Without as much as a twitch, Titonius said, "It appears that my son has returned to me. Though, in what state he is remains to be seen."

"Father, I seek your forgiveness for my abrupt departure. The sheep's hand had no right to disagree with your proposal, which was right and just. And then the clothes merchants voice grated upon my last nerves. I tried my meditation exercise, but with every count, I just wanted to throw my knife at him to make him stop talking. I also tried to project an aura of silence and calm, but I am afraid that I wasn't successful at that either."

In one motion, Titonius stood and turned to face his son. His amethyst eyes peered deeply into Uriel's, and he strode toward the temple entrance. "My son, it is only expected that you experience many failures before you succumb to success. It is said that Atlantis wasn't raised in a day. And neither did I rise to the Kingship in a day. Patience. That is what we will meditate upon. Patience. Let us retire to your mother and home." He brushed the matter and dust off his breeches, turned and walked out of the temple. Uriel followed behind, carefully studying his feet. As they exited the temple, the people nodded their heads in reverence to the King and his son.

Personal Essay
Final Judge — Chip Livingston
Montevideo, Uruguay

First Place
The Fire
Leigh Watson Healy
Havana, Florida

Shattering glass disturbed me on that sweltering summer night, but the humming air conditioner lulled me back to sleep. I was alone in our apartment across from Atlanta's Piedmont Park, while John was playing a gig and not due home until the early morning hours. Crashing glass again. Still foggy from sleep, I thought there had been another car wreck on that busy road on a Friday night. More splintering sounds, and now I was wide awake.

Everything was fine in our apartment: lights on, air conditioner running, all normal. I trudged to the sunporch off the bedroom and peered out, cranking open the jalousie window to listen and to get a better view. More crashing sounds and then shouts: "Fire! Get out!" The building next door must be on fire. Pulling on jeans, grabbing my wallet and keys, I opened the front door without feeling first to see if it was hot. Beyond the door, the hallway was another world. The lights were out; the stair landing was dark. Dim light ghosted through the stairwell windows.

First locking the door, I ran down the smoky stairway, burst through the door, and found a throng of people on the street. I hadn't heard the firefighters pounding on my door earlier; I was the last one to escape the building.

The fire had begun on the floor below ours where a couple was running a restaurant in their apartment. Fire crews battled the blaze as it burned in the basement, the first floor, and then up through the walls. Flames burst through the third-story windows. Now the entire roof was on fire, and every window glowed like jack-o'-lantern eyes. Black smoke obscured the night sky.

The hill across the road became a theatre where I sat with everyone watching our building burn.

John got through the roadblocks up the street and found me. We wondered whether everyone was all right. Dancers lived on the third floor, and they were out of town on tour, we hoped. I thought of our wedding pictures and the box of my great grandmother's handmade lace. John wanted to rescue the baby grand piano my grandparents had given our family when I was a child.

We sipped coffee supplied by the Red Cross and thanked them for the $100 they handed out for necessities and a place to stay the night. We crashed at a friend's house with the clothes on our backs.

Two days later, we went to see what we could salvage after the looters took what they wanted. Dad had said we should hire a security guard to watch our apartment. We didn't. Odd things had disappeared from our sooty, water-soaked rooms. Taken was a taxidermy owl left with us by a friend passing through. The fridge was missing a leftover bottle of wine. The blender sat full of dingy water, with its lid still in place. Bookshelves held soggy art books with coated paper pages glued shut. The old chandelier had crashed through the glass-topped table in the dining room. Sooty water filled the piano.

Only a week later, we moved into our first house. The fire

made the move easy—we brought a mattress and a few items of clothing. Creative people—dancers, artists, and musicians—lived in our Arts and Crafts-era apartment building. Everyone struggled to get by. No one could afford insurance, and most people lost everything. We were lucky. Everyone was lucky. No one got hurt; no one lost life. With blue sky and puffy clouds showing through the demolished roof, we began again with fewer possessions to take care of and our lives ahead of us.

Second Place
As We Forgive Our Debtors
Richard Key
Dothan, Alabama

My bicycle was stolen last year, on top of everything else. I loved that bike, an $800 Specialized with a black frame and super smooth gear shifting. I got it as a Christmas gift from my wife a few years ago and, when not in use, kept it in the garage locked up tight. The crime occurred at Callaway Gardens, a family-oriented park with asphalt bike trails connecting areas of interest, including a couple of lakes. I went alone, ironically, taking the advice of many to get outside in nature to counteract the negativity of isolation. The park was fairly busy for a weekday. I didn't expect as many other people to be out counteracting their own isolation negativity. Mistake number one.

It happened like this: I decided to pop into the Cecil B. Day Butterfly Center for a minute or two and watch the butterflies flit around. Yes, and to use the facilities—do I have to say that? I didn't bring a bike lock with me since I didn't think I'd be stopping long enough for anyone to conceive, much less carry out, a felony (mistake number two). And besides, it's a family-oriented place. One shouldn't have to bolt everything to bedrock to retain possession, should they? Also, I reasoned, if there were any criminals there, you'd think apple dumpling gang sort of people.

But the bike was gone when I came back out. Not a trace, not a tire mark or anything. I had parked it in an out-of-the-way area so it would not be so noticeable, which obviously was another error in judgment. Even if I'd caught a glimpse of the thief, which I didn't, a pursuit on foot would have been futile. All I could do was contact Security.

"In the two years I've been here, I've never heard of anyone's bike getting stolen," the young security officer told me after he picked me up to take me back to my car. "Maybe we'll find it abandoned somewhere."

If it was abandoned anywhere, it was on eBay or Craig's list. I never heard back from the guy after I spent twenty-five minutes filing a report.

But here is the uplifting part of the story: I have totally forgiven this person, this probable male in his teens or early twenties, who no doubt squanders his sorry life away playing Grand Theft Auto on his stolen laptop.

Yes, I have asked God to forgive him completely. I pray that when this perpetrator, who got off scot free, is involved in an accident where he is blind-sided by a truck, that it not be fatal. Semi-fatal is just fine. When the first responders arrive, I hope fervently that the rescue tools used to pry his mangled body from the wreckage don't inadvertently cause permanent nerve damage.

And when he is lying in the operating room waiting for the medical team to arrive, that the bacteria infecting his compound fractures be, at least initially, sensitive to common antibiotics. And that the neurosurgeon, called in from a party to treat his subdural hematoma, has a fairly low blood alcohol level, given the circumstances, and doesn't drill the burr holes too deep into the skull such that pink brain tissue begins to ooze out leaving him unable to spell the word *cat*.

And that the piece of his pelvis bone removed to reshape his jaw doesn't leave such a defect that his gait is forever altered. And that the blood transfusion he receives during surgery isn't accidentally typed wrong so that he has a transfusion reaction. And when he is recovering from surgery, that a poorly-trained nurse doesn't confuse the room numbers and administer an enema that wasn't ordered. And that he doesn't trip over any objects left on the floor during his rehabilitation causing his progress to be set back two months.

On my way out of the park I returned to the scene of the crime on the off chance that the thief had a change of heart, a pang of conscience, and took the bike back to where he stole it. But no such luck.

So began a bike-less period that lasted almost four months. During which time I imagined the remorseless felon shifting those seamless gears over hill and valley, coasting freely in the warm spring air, oblivious to trucks speeding down perpendicular roads toward him.

I hope to God nothing happens.

Third Place
Dad's Grief
Leigh Watson Healy
Havana, Florida

It was still dark as I crept downstairs from the stuffy guest bedroom, cringing as I passed under the impala head mounted in the stairwell. As expected, Dad was in the sitting room, in his favorite leather chair, feet on the needlepoint footstool that he had ever since I could remember.

He had a newspaper open and others waiting to be read or in disarray on the floor.

"Morning, Dad," I said.

He said, "Hi there, honey. Get some coffee and come sit with me."

I fetched a mug from the kitchen and sat in the twin chair by the reading lamp. Bea and the yappy dog would sleep late. On visits like this, I loved these rare times when I had Dad to myself.

Still waking up, I gazed through the double doors into the living room and took in the decor of that seldom-used space. The room glittered. Gilt and crystals were everywhere, on candlesticks, lamps and breakables, and on shelves, the étagère, and tabletops. "Be careful. Don't spill anything on the rugs," sounded in my head. The rugs included a bear skin complete with claws and growling mouth. A tiger skin draped over the piano. Big game animal heads hung on the walls, trophies from African safaris with her second husband, as they helicopted in to find the best animals to shoot. Glass-topped display tables–reliquaries enshrining objects from her second marriage–were full of little, fragile things: figurines, carvings, jeweled eggs, geodes, and other no-touch items.

As I sipped coffee, I thought about how Dad ended up in this place, Bea's house. My dad, who, when friends would invite him on quail hunting trips, could never bring himself to pull the trigger. Who thought sailboat racing was excellent sport and whose idea of shooting was photographing his travels to exotic locations. Who, with Mim, was a patron of the arts and libraries. Who in the last year of his life, bought himself only a fresh pair of Hush Puppies slippers, while Bea shopped for furs.

How did he get here? First, there was marriage to my mom, a union that collapsed while I was at college, although trouble began years earlier. Mim, Dad's second wife, was the genuine love of his life. They had twenty-four blissful years together before a brain tumor took her. Bea brought her famous mac and cheese to Mim's wake. One day, Dad surprised me when he called to say, "Bea and I are getting married and want you all to come to the wedding."

"Wait, Bea who?" I said. Dad married Bea only eighteen months after Mim died.

So, they wed, and he moved into her house. There was no room for him to bring much of his own things. Now here, at home with Bea, Dad had his reading chair and footstool, the desk in his study, and in the bedroom, his dresser. Later, after he died, I found buried in the bottom drawer of that dresser a little box that had Mim's driver license, passport, their wedding rings, and photos and other mementos of her. Another box held her treasured bookbinding tools.

Yet, when he married Bea, Dad worked hard on bringing our fractured family into a relationship with Bea's family. He continued to nurture and support Mim's children and grandchildren. The year they married, he organized a Rhine

River cruise for us all to get to know and love Bea. A few years later, he hosted us all on a Christmas cruise to Mexico, planned a year ahead to ensure we had a lovely holiday together. He wanted us to be one family.

I snapped out of my thoughts when Dad put down his paper, drew in his breath, and let out a deep sigh. Looking straight ahead, he said, "I miss her so much." The best talks I had with Dad always happened like this: his eyes straight ahead, hands on the wheel as he drove wherever we were going, just the two of us talking. Or like today, sitting together before the world was awake. He looked at me, his eyes swimming in tears. "Did I do the right thing marrying Bea? What would Mim think? Would she approve? I miss her so."

"Dad," I said, "Mim loved you so much and wanted you to be happy. I'm sure she's up there chuckling that you married her good friend and wondering if it was the mac and cheese that did the trick. She would be glad to know that you are not alone."

We sat like this for a little while, and I squeezed his hand. Dad cleared his throat with a couple of little coughs. Then he picked up the newspaper and began reading again, eyes straight ahead.

Nonfiction
Final Judge — Dr. Cheryl Jennings
Tallahassee, Florida

First Place
Missing Hands
Faith Eidse
Tallahassee, Florida

Mukedi mission was built in 1923 along a Congo ridge overlooking a wooded valley and snaking river. Its houses were cavernous with quarried stone walls, tin roofs and soaring ceilings. Bordered by bright zinnias, they seemed like decorated castles. Four American families and several single women worked in the clinic and school and visited over potluck.

I had come to stay with Jette, another third grader, in a homeschool exchange. On days off, her dad, Pete Buller, the secondary school director, played hide-and-seek or tag with us kids. Most days, Jette's little brother Chuck tore around on his red tricycle, carrying village friends or letting them pedal while he ran alongside. He was the sharingest five-year-old I knew.

I felt like a princess moving into Jette's huge bedroom, which she shared with Chuck. Aunt Gladys had assured my parents that I would be safe. "Our Africans won't let us starve." I wasn't sure the Africans wanted to be owned that way, but I also knew their shared love and the law of the village—you divided your last manioc mush with your neighbors.

From Jette's bedroom, wooden shutters opened onto a fenced backyard that had everything you'd expect in an American playground—merry-go-round, seesaw, swings. Beneath the high pink of having it all was the dark feeling of having too much. How could villagers not be jealous of this?

The grownups discussed how the Congo's former minister of education, Mulele Pierre, was getting most of his followers from this area. They saw how, after fighting for independence, others had moved into privileged Belgian roles, leaving them behind. The Phende had been oppressed, put down and had only received a few seats in local parliament.

Among the things I missed my first days away from home in Kamayala were my mother's soft cheek and daily outings with my three sisters and friends to the river. In a matter of days, I had become more separated from Africa than I could imagine. When the village mamas crossed Jette's yard with water pails and bowls of laundry, I begged to go along.

The Bullers knew more than we did about the Jeunesse—youth revolutionaries—and they were nervous about letting us out of the fenced yard. But finally, Aunt Gladys agreed to let us follow the women, as long as we stayed close to them.

We descended through flowing grasslands, muddy hardwood forests, and plunged into the river—cool, brown-stained, sweet and woodsy on the tongue. While we swam, the women pounded laundry on rocks, filled gourds and beckoned us uphill again.

Mulele had set up a command post just six miles away and was promising change, a caring government, a better life. The name "Mulele" was on every lip, his anthem sung as though the black Messiah had come.

For Geography, we went to Charles Sprunger's cinder block bungalow where his wife Aunt Geraldine taught us to draw maps and ask questions about how different people lived. She had two preschoolers and worried about what had happened to their dad who was supposed to deliver a transmitter to

Kandale. No transmitter had yet crackled on the airwaves, and we had no way of knowing that he had been taken hostage, marched 70 kilometers and held before Jeunesse tribunals.

We knew how close the revolution had come when the Bullers' cook came to work one Monday, eyes droopy, wearing a cloth wrapper instead of Western trousers. Had he spent the weekend with Mulele in the forest learning guerilla warfare?

On Thursday morning, January 23, 1964, the front door shook with urgent knocking. *"Ko-ko-ko!"*

I padded through slatted light to the master bedroom but hesitated to wake Aunt Gladys, a tall, regal woman who liked her beauty sleep.

I raced back to the bedroom. "Jette. Wake up."

Jette sat up, hair frizzy. "What? Are the rebels here?"

People came to the door all the time. Sometimes they were kids wanting to ride Chuck's tricycle. So, instead of waking her parents, Jette and I zipped to the door and opened it a crack. A dark, muscled man trembled there in white shirt and blue shorts, eyes wide, sweat pouring from his face. He spoke rapidly in Giphende and handed us a note.

In the yard, the neighbor, Dr. Nickel, called, "Pete, it's an emergency."

Uncle Pete came from the bedroom buttoning his shirt, reached over us, took the note and stepped outside.

We learned later, it was a plea for help from the neighboring Catholic mission, Kilembe, delivered by their school director. The Mother Superior wrote, "Sirs, Please come over and help us. Last night all the priests at the mission were massacred. Terrible! Please come get us to take us, if possible, on to Idiofa" (a Catholic mission 70 miles north).

Outside, voices were urgent—priests chopped "kyaa," their

jeeps burned. The school director had run—with the note—under a hail of arrows.

Uncle Pete crossed the rug, bumping into tow-headed Chuck. We crowded around the bedroom door, but Aunt Gladys was already tying on a robe, reaching to shut the door. "Children to the living room." In minutes, Mr. Buller raced past us with pickup keys jangling, stopped for Dr. Nickel and drove off the station.

We sat on the rug and planned our escape—a game we'd played for weeks. We'd cut through the yard to the river jungle where we could hide and drink from the river.

"We can take our blankets." Jette started the take-along list.

"Okay, small blankets." I had learned from big sister Hope to be practical. "One each but no pillows—too big."

"We can take sardines." Jette brightened. "They come with keys attached for opening."

"Sure okay—fine—in our pillowcases."

"I'm going to take my trike!" Chuck pedaled madly around the rug, ghostly rebels in hot pursuit.

"How are we supposed to carry it when we leave the path?" I was practiced.

"Put it in a barrel."

"How are we supposed to carry the barrel?" Jette grinned at me.

"Just roll it down the hill."

Jette and I laughed. It was almost as though we could slip into the grass, wait for the rebels to march past, then emerge as if from a camping trip, to take back our beds, clothes and toys. We did not understand the finality of that morning. It would be the last time for months we'd be surrounded by familiar things—rugs, sofas, tricycles. The last time for weeks our lives would feel like our own. The last time for years that missionaries would live in the grand houses of Mukedi.

Aunt Gladys came from the bedroom, buttoning her dress, headed in several directions at once. At the bathroom door, traveling case in hand, Aunt Gladys turned to us still in our pajamas. "Children, get dressed. Harvey's radioing for evacuation. I'm packing a few things we need. You can each take a change of clothing, a favorite toy and book."

The Harvey Barkmans were a family from our area of Manitoba, Canada. They'd look out for us. At the bureau drawer I fingered several pairs of bright print shorts and tops sewed by Aunt Gladys. They were my first ever, and I wasn't finished wearing them yet. But if we were fleeing Mukedi, I'd be going back to my family where shorts weren't proper for girls.

I went to the closet, instead, chose my best pink Sunday dress and folded it into the zipper skirt of my pajama doll, Polly—named for Pollyanna—a story my parents loved about always looking on the bright side. Polly, with her plastic smile, was a gift from them for traveling, perfect for facing the unknown.

From the night stand, I added my Bible—a sacred protection—shield against arrows. From the bureau drawer, a pair of socks and underwear. That was all. I left notebooks, pencils, an American geography book and reader.

"Jette? Chuck?" Aunt Gladys walked into the room. "Faith? Are you packed? Rebels burned the Catholic mission last night. We don't think they'll come here, but we're leaving just in case."

What if they did? Would they cut us with machetes? I didn't ask these questions aloud. The internal soft pedal was down. I didn't want to be too much trouble. It was possible we wouldn't get away at all. I might not see Hope, Charity, Grace, or Mom and Dad, again.

What if the plane was too small? What if we overloaded, crashed and burned? What if I had to wait for another flight? My own parents weren't here, and if it came to grabbing children, wouldn't any parent grab theirs first? Maybe I had separated too easily from my parents, had wanted too much to escape the daily drill at home—clear the table, comb your hair, stand up straight. At the moment, that dull, predictable routine seemed the best life ever.

Aunt Gladys circled the room, touched a handmade doll, a batik hanging—crafts she'd made with her sewing classes. She was my substitute mother and her caring touch reassured me. "The planes are on their way. The youngest mothers and children will go first. Then the rest of the women and children—that's us."

"What about the dads?" Chuck was totally identified with his dad.

"They'll get out." Aunt Gladys's voice seemed strained. "We'll all get out. Don't worry, honey."

"What about my family?" I barely dared ask.

Aunt Gladys had grey moons under her eyes. "The pilots say the countryside is on fire. Everyone is leaving."

I shadowed Aunt Gladys who raced around, looking through desk drawers, stuffing papers, passports and cash into her handbag. Perhaps she worried whether she'd see her ten-year-old son, James, again—away at school. There was no telling what the students were hearing or fearing.

In the kitchen, the cook scowled over a sink full of dishes. Aunt Gladys spoke to him in short words, and he answered in shorter ones. Aunt Gladys backed up and stepped on my toes. She threw up her hands. "Outside! Children, outside. Go watch for the plane."

Yikes, I had made her send us out into the open—by being too clingy. I had to use more control.

The Bullers' house was at the end of the road, so we were near the high grass if we had to run. We twirled on the merry-go-round, checked the grass for arrows and clutched our Bibles like shields. We sang choruses as though music itself were a weapon. "I stand alone on the word of God..." Louder. Stronger. Faster.

Dizzy with spinning, dizzy with fear. Maybe if we spun fast enough, we'd blur out, turn to vapor and the arrows wouldn't hit us. We took turns pushing the merry-go-round, our thin legs pounding the ground. Harder, harder. The Jeunesse were coming. Faster, faster. Until our lungs burst. We flopped onto the seat, heads back, the sky spinning, filling with a toy plane that grew larger through the mango canopy.

"Airplane!" We shouted and ran out the gate.

"Where do you think you're going?" Aunt Gladys stood on the kitchen doorstep.

"The plane—"

"That is not our plane. That one's for the babies—besides, we're not walking to the airstrip. It's not safe."

The pilot had radioed that a band of shirtless men with bows and arrows was headed to the airstrip. "Call off the fighting. I don't want to be a pin cushion."

My stomach felt like raw eggs slipping on grease. I was one person too many, pushing us to wait for the next plane with the Jeunesse already here. Would we all get out alive?

Mukedi's Chief Nzamba arrived with his twelve sons, all

with shotguns, and sent the Jeunesse into the tall grass. His people had his ear, but he also wanted to preserve Mukedi. He and his sons strode between the rebels and the airstrip so the evacuations could continue.

Mr. Buller had returned from the Catholic station with six nuns and a Belgian teacher in the back of the pickup and we went to Dr. Nickel's house to gather around them.

Dr. Nickel and Mr. Buller had helped bury the priests in a shallow grave. The doctor had noticed the bloody cast of the priest whose leg he'd set the Sunday before. The leg had been re-broken, and the priests had been hacked with machetes, some of their hands and fingers missing.

Seven women, six in habits as white as their faces, stood around the Nickels' stone fireplace. The crinkle-eyed Mother Superior hovered over the young, shaken teacher. She told in French how the church's tin roof was pelted with stones, and they'd huddled in the locked back office. Even after Mr. Buller had driven them into Mukedi, they were threatened by men running along the road.

While they stood there, a man entered the house and said he was sent to kill them but would spare them if they paid him. Nowhere were they safe. The women huddled and took a collection for him. One nun cradled a newborn whose mother had died at their clinic the night before. "We'll take her with us from here." We waited behind locked doors, drawn curtains.

Mr. Buller left to radio for help from Idiofa. The mood had turned against the Europeans, especially the Belgians. Would the Americans be next? Mr. Buller spoke with a mission leader who said the missionaries must leave. Women and children first, then men. The fighting was beyond their control.

The buzz of a second plane opened overhead. The pickup

bounced up to the back door. "This is your plane!" Mr. Buller grabbed Aunt Gladys's case and hurried us into the truck. "Wes Eiseman buzzed Kandale, and their homes are burned but the missionaries are all alive. The mission is trying to get UN helicopters to rescue them."

I clutched my fuzzy pink Polly over the bumpy road to the airstrip. The truck braked beside a yellow single-prop plane. Avril Barkman, her son Lowell and midwife Elda Hiebert were already huddled under the wing—seven people to be squeezed into three seats.

"Adults first." Gordon Fairly, pilot of the second flight, placed our few bags in the cargo hold and assigned the women to the three passenger seats and the children one or two to a lap. He scanned the sky. A Congo army plane had circled over the first evacuation flight and several Phende men had threatened Mr. Buller. "You called the army!" They sliced fingers across their throats. "If that plane lands, we'll kill you."

"Kill me if you must. But I didn't call the army."

Mr. Eiseman had flung open his window and shouted over the engine howl. "Get that truck in the middle of the airstrip!"

Mr. Barkman jumped into the pickup and raced onto the runway.

The army plane descended, landing gear lowered and headed straight for the truck. Mr. Barkman leaned on his horn. The army plane dipped as if to demolish him but pulled up within inches. One more time the plane circled and then veered off.

"The army better not try that again." Mr. Fairly cut short our good-byes and closed the door between fathers and families.

"Yay the army!" said Chuck.

"Not yay," Aunt Gladys said. "If the army returns, there'll

be all out war."

"I hope Harvey gets out okay." Mrs. Barkman clutched Lowell on her lap. Her daughter Sandra and son Gerald were away at school, too. What had they heard?

Mr. Fairly radioed for takeoff. He revved the engine, dust flew, and the fathers stepped back against the grass — where men hid with arrows nocked. Everyone looked at the dads who nodded back with solemn eyes, grim smiles, raised hands.

The pilot released the brakes and launched the plane down the runway.

I shifted on Ms. Hiebert's lap, my head wedged against the ceiling.

"You're going to have to sit very still." She spoke firmly. "You don't have a seat belt."

The loaded plane lumbered downhill toward high grass and trees. I held myself high and light, knuckles white on the seat in front of me. It didn't seem near fast enough to break free. We hovered too long over high grass and scrub brush. At last the plane nosed up, shaving treetops. A hundred feet below, the airstrip fell away and with it the fathers, waving.

Mr. Buller had raised the shrouds that covered the priests before laying them in a shallow grave. There was only time to throw shovels of dirt on top and wonder whether the missing digits and hands were cured and eaten for power at ceremonies in the forest.

But Mulele's actions may have been more symbolic than that. Before independence, he had been conscripted into the *Force Publique,* Belgium's army since King Leopold II had staked out the Congo Free State in the 1880s. Mulele had investigated official reports of raids on villages that fell behind in rubber quotas: summary executions, women and children captured, hands severed. Or, by proxy, children's hands and feet taken. Mulele may have seen photos—baskets full of shrunken hands—a colonial currency delivered by soldiers for bonus pay.

Kilembe was within the borders of the Congo Free State and Mulele may have known maimed elders, grandmas of his own clan. The children with missing hands were my grandma's age, born in my century.

Idiofa could not supply a plane, so the fathers put the nuns on the next two flights and waited hours for their rescue plane. Chief Nzamba and sons paced. He had advised them to get out before Mulele arrived and issued orders.

Finally, the last flight arrived, the pilot lost for hours over a smoky countryside, blown off course by a strong north wind. The flight to Kikwit followed the setting sun into tropical night. Behind them, Jeunesse arrived with whetted machetes. "We got the priests. Where are the Protestants? We have to kill at least one Protestant."

Second Place
Family Banishment
Doug Alderson
Tallahassee, Florida

Behind the Denny's. That's where James said to meet him. He had sounded desperate on the phone. "I'm tired of getting pushed around, being taken advantage of. I lost it and had an altercation. Now, a gang is after me. I need to get out of here, need to get off the streets tonight."

James was the boyfriend of Melody, my second cousin. Both had been on the streets for almost a year. Melody needed psychiatric care, but always refused help. When she would call me for financial help, it was difficult to discern truth from fiction. James was more of a straight talker, more believable and to the point. And sometimes in trouble.

I stepped out of my silver Prius and scanned the parking area. Behind Denny's was a car stereo store; a figure standing in the shadows stepped out. Was that James? He was dressed in black and wearing a black mask, not completely unusual since the pandemic was still raging. I could make out a slightly built black man, but that was about it.

He did a half wave and approached me, looking very ninja like with a machete at his side. A long gleaming machete. How well did I know James? Background information was sketchy. I knew he had been in prison for a meth conviction, he had a daughter in another state, and he and Melody had been together off and on for years. He did sporadic day labor for money and once worked at a Waffle House, although he now lacked legal identification to get a real job, something about his birth certificate and social security card being tied up with his dysfunctional family. He had no driver's license. James was usually soft-spoken and low key, but even mellow people have their breaking points.

James had more street smarts than Melody because she had carried over lifestyle and clothing preferences from her wealthy West Coast upbringing. Her father, my first cousin, had co-founded a successful business, sold it for millions and retired to a plush lake house in another state. He and Melody were often at odds, she getting into drugs and alcohol as a young teen and generally running with the wrong crowd for the next 40 years. Finally, about a year before, there was a family blowout and Melody's parents essentially banished her, cut off all financial support and contact. So, at age 57, Melody was completely on her own for the first time—no free house, no car, and nary any job experience or motivation to get a job. But she had James, someone who knew how to scratch and claw for a living and help Melody survive, if only she would listen.

"Hey Doug," James said softly, keeping the machete half hidden behind his leg as he slowly approached, glancing around.

"You okay, James?"

"Yeah, but Melody is going to get me killed."

I didn't pry into this latest incident. There had been others, especially after Melody had been attacked on the street and robbed of her cell phone while James was out working. That prompted a two-day trip to the hospital where Melody received stiches to the head and was diagnosed with a concussion. Afterwards, she shook and cried while clutching her bible. "My father has given me a death sentence!"

She had had a similar rant when a brown recluse bit her while she was sleeping outside. "Why would any parent allow their child to go through such a thing!" I wanted to tell her that age 57 was a good point in life to stop blaming your parents for your troubles, but I kept silent. She was too upset.

"Where is she?" I asked James.

"She's always wandering off, panhandling somewhere. I told her to be back here by now, but I have no idea where she is."

James would often vent about Melody when she wasn't around. Living with her, especially on the street, must be frustrating. He needed to vent or he would blow, and sometimes he did. But I also knew he loved her. He once told me he tried to leave her during one of her panic-filled episodes where she accused him of being an agent of her father whose job was to make her fail. But he could only stay away for a couple of hours. He loved her and knew she needed him.

I glanced up and down Monroe Street, one of Tallahassee's busiest thoroughfares, but no Melody. Melody had once beseeched me to take them both in, put them up indefinitely, but I lived ten miles out of town in a small house with my wife and had no extra bedroom. She and James would have to camp out in our living room with no viable transportation of their own. I would constantly be running Melody to the store for booze and cigarettes and be handed divorce papers by my wife within a month. So, despite being wracked with guilt for not taking in a homeless family member, I could only dole out occasional cash and food. No other family member wanted two permanent house guests with issues either, especially since reports had circulated about items disappearing wherever Melody stayed, pawnable items. Her own parents had filed a no trespass order and warned family members to stay clear. But Melody and James had made their way to Tallahassee and kept calling, begging even.

Out of frustration, I once communicated with Melody's father to see if we could figure out a long-term solution together. I always found him to be logical and reasonable, and family oriented. "We have come to the conclusion that Melody is seriously delusional, paranoid and mentally ill," be began. "We have encouraged her to seek treatment in a professional facility, but I doubt she will ever do that. We would hate to see you or other family members get involved with her. Every time we try to help, it doesn't end well. It's not possible to help someone who refuses to help themselves. What a sad situation and a waste of a life by someone who had every opportunity."

That summed up Melody pretty well, except I had also known her to be generous, someone who took in stray dogs and people. James, an ex-con on the streets, had been one of those strays, but now Melody needed James more than the other way around.

"I got 10 dollars to my name," James said, his eyes bloodshot. I believed him. Melody would have hit me up for money even if she had a hundred dollars in her purse, but James had once refused help because he had some "pocket money." He never pushed it.

"I can spare eighty bucks today," I said. "Enough for a motel room and some food."

James seemed to relax. "Thanks, that will be a big help."

We walked back to the car stereo store and it was then that I noticed a shopping cart at the back of the building piled high with suitcases and backpacks along with another giant suitcase beside it. "Is all of that yours?" I asked. Their belongings had multiplied since the last time I saw them.

James stuck the machete part-way into the ground beside the

shopping cart. "It's mostly Melody's, mostly her clothes. She's got another full cart behind the dumpster, but stuff got wet and it smells bad. She can't let go of anything."

"All of that stuff won't fit in my car."

"I know."

I handed James the eighty bucks. "This is all I can do for now. I can't pay for another room tomorrow." I had always made it clear I couldn't give cash every day, taking a lesson from my younger brother who had generously helped Melody and James for months until he realized Melody would hit him up for money even when she didn't need it. She was a con artist, he concluded. My brother had even given them a good, working, used vehicle, which they promptly traded in for a bomb so they could get extra cash from the deal. The cash quickly ran out, their vehicle became hopelessly inoperable, and that was that. It proved her father's conclusion that efforts to help Melody never worked out. My brother became burned out, tired of being viewed as an ATM, so Melody turned her attention to other family members and a few friends. Between Melody's hustling and panhandling and James's odd jobs, they rotated back and forth from sleeping in a homeless camp near Interstate 10 and staying in a motel.

City shelters were not an option. The sudden influx of unemployed people on the streets because of the pandemic had created a homeless crisis. But even when temporary shelters would be offered by the city when temperatures dropped below 35 degrees, Melody refused because that meant she and James would be separated. "You can't trust people at the shelters," she told me. James said she was too picky, but he usually went along when she insisted. She was the alpha in the relationship.

James put the four twenty-dollar bills in his pocket. He

glanced up Monroe Street. "Where the hell is she?" He sighed. "Now, I don't want to keep you, Doug. The motel isn't far. We can roll this cart and the big suitcase there."

I didn't argue with him. Darkness was falling, temperatures were dropping, and since I couldn't fit all of their stuff in my car anyway—along with that machete—what more could I do? Plus, there was the pandemic to think about.

When I pulled out of Denny's and onto Monroe Street, I spotted Melody walking toward Denny's on the sidewalk. She had a box of takeout food in her hand, a pleased look on her face, wearing the stylish coat she admitted she had stolen from a Goodwill because she didn't have fourteen dollars. Her first theft, she claimed. She was the granddaughter of a cherished aunt, the great-granddaughter of my warm-hearted grandmother. Were they now scolding me from the afterlife for not doing more? She was family. But she was Melody. And she had been banished.

Third Place
Moon Matters
Richard Key
Dothan, Alabama

Here's a fun fact: Both moons of the planet Mars would easily fit into many of our national parks. Instead of moon rocks, there would be actual moons that folks could come by and gawk at. Both could actually be squeezed into Lake Tahoe or Lake Pontchartrain, too, although they would project considerably above the surface. The smaller, Deimos, is almost eight miles across and the other, Phobos, is just less than fourteen miles wide. Neither, of course, is likely to end up in any park or in one of Earth's lakes, so New Orleans needn't be worried about getting flooded again. It's merely an illustration.

Our beloved moon, by comparison, is 2,158 miles in diameter. That's 17, 264 furlongs, if that's what you go by. But regardless of the units, it is fifth largest of the 214 known planetary moons. The largest is Jupiter's moon Ganymede, named, as all of Jupiter's moons are, for the Roman god Jupiter's mythological lovers and besties.

Ganymede is about a thousand miles larger in diameter than our moon. The other moons larger than Earth's moon are Jupiter's Callisto and Io, and Saturn's Titan. Ganymede and Titan are, surprisingly, larger than the planet Mercury. Let that sink in—moons that are larger than the smallest planet. And much larger than demoted Pluto, which is now classified as a "dwarf planet" and was last seen living under a bridge in the nether reaches of the solar system.

Jupiter has the most moons. Back when I was in school, we were informed that Jupiter had twelve moons and Saturn had nine, which sounded as factual as any of the stuff we had to memorize. But the actual updated figure for both is dozens—seventy-nine for Jupiter and sixty-two for Saturn. Both have exactly fifty-three named moons. Twenty-six of Jupiter's moons and nine of Saturn's moons are "provisional" which means they are waiting to be confirmed by additional data before being given official names. With so many moons up in the sky, nursery rhymes on these large planets have a bewildering choice of which one to have the cow to jump over.

There is a committee of some distinction that determines the names of planetary moons. It's called the IAU, the International Astronomical Union, made up of almost 12,000 active professional astronomers representing more than 100 countries. According to their website, the IAU "serves as the internationally recognized authority for assigning designations to celestial bodies and the surface features on them."

The job of naming moons, then, involves more than flipping through the index of mythology books looking for catchy names that haven't been taken yet. There apparently needs to be some theme, internal consistency, and a certain amount of agreement among the astronomers who vote. But the truth is, when it comes to the name of an obscure moon circling a distant planet, almost anything would suffice. Two moons could have the same name and who's going to notice—Ken Jennings? IBM's Watson?

With Jupiter, the experts may have already run through the list of the god's mythological romantic partners, favored daughters, and cupbearers. And old roommates, beloved nannies, and housekeepers. All that's left are the mythological former neighbors, yardmen, chiropractors, and the guy at Seven Eleven that sold him lottery tickets every Wednesday.

In Saturn's case, the moons already have to compete with those gaudy rings. Saturn doesn't really need any moons, does it? It's too much bling in my opinion. Saturn is the Zsa Zsa's jewelry box of the solar system.

In case you need a refresher course in Roman mythology, here's a brief summary. Saturn overthrew his father Caelus, the supreme sky god, to become number one. He subsequently learned of a prophecy foretelling his downfall at the hands of one of his children. So, one by one, as each of his first five children by wife Ops are born, he swallows them. Ops hides number six—Jupiter—and tricks her husband into swallowing a stone disguised as a baby. Saturn, unable to digest the rock, regurgitates it along with the first five offspring (Ceres, Juno, Neptune, Pluto, and Vesta). Jupiter then conspires with them to overthrow their father, thus becoming the new number one.

Jupiter's brothers, Neptune and Pluto, lent their names to planets, of course, and his son, Mars, also. Jupiter was married to one sister, Juno, and had an affair with another sister, Ceres, with whom he sired Proserpine. Affairs with non-sisters Maia, goddess of earth and fertility, and Dione yielded Mercury and Venus respectively. So, there is the sordid and complicated family history of the planets in a nutshell.

Uranus seems like the outlier as the only planet named for a Greek god. But Uranus is the Greek equivalent of Caelus, the supreme sky god in Roman mythology whom Saturn overthrew. The circle is thus complete, at least in the zany world of ancient mythology. It makes keeping up with the Kardashians seem simple by comparison.

Mercury and Venus have no moons at all. Nothing at all to gaze up at in the night sky, except stars. There's Earth, of course, a bluish dot with a tiny little moon next to it. You might

2022 Seven Hills Review

be able to see that with a pair of binoculars as you try to keep from being cooked alive or frozen. But no satellite to call their own. I suppose we could start a GoFundMe page to champion the cause—moonsformercury.com, for instance.

Which leaves Uranus and Neptune, the outermost planets. Neptune is known to have "at least" fourteen moons. It turns out the number of moons for several of the planets has been difficult to pin down. Some moons are very far away from the planet they orbit. Others are incorporated into rings, and some have simply been lost in the crowd. The entire business of moon counting is a work in progress.

The largest of Neptune's moons is named Triton, not to be confused with Saturn's moon Titan, or Uranus's Titania. You might be able to predict what Neptune's moons are named for. Since Neptune was the god of the sea, the moons are named for lesser sea gods and nymphs, like Hippocamp, Nereid, and Neso.

Uranus has twenty-seven moons—all officially named for characters from Shakespeare plays and Alexander Pope's mock epic poem "The Rape of the Lock" about a stolen lock of character Belinda's hair. So, there is a moon named Belinda circling Uranus, as well as a Margaret. And there is also a Juliet, but, alas, no Romeo. The smallest moon of Uranus is Cupid, at eleven miles across also small enough to fit into many of Earth's lakes and reservoirs.

You might be wondering *what's the deal with trying to stuff moons into lakes*? The author just happens to be fascinated with the idea of tiny moons, that's all. It's nothing psychological—at least not yet. In fact, there are something like thirty moons circling other planets that could easily fit into many of our lakes. The two smallest, both orbiting Saturn, are petite enough to fit into some large farm ponds. The smallest, S2009/S-1 (the provisional name until the IAU comes up with something better), at 500 feet, is not much bigger than a football field.

In summary, reviewing the current situation of planetary moons in our solar system may renew the reader's appreciation for our one beloved moon, Luna. One moon is sufficient in my opinion, certainly when it comes to nursery rhymes, eclipses, manned space missions, and hitting someone in the eye like a big pizza pie. Life on Earth is complex enough as it is.

THE PENUMBRA POETRY AND
HAIKU COMPETITION

Poetry
Final Judge—Benjamin Dugger
Elizabethton, Tennessee

First Place
Paradise, California 11/08/2018
Bob Gibbs
Tallahassee, Florida

This is a shape poem. To get it to fit on the page, we turned it on its side and printed it on the next page. Read the poem from the last line on the right (bottom of the poem) to the first line on the left (top of the poem).

I am God, the devastating judgment, the unholy provoker of death and destruction. Call me Wildfire!
Now, in control, I will lay waste to this unprotected planet before the flooding oceans can do the job.
Gnats, frogs, a bloody river, amateurish; with that dry desert and winds I could have been a star.
This wimpy God only wanted to get their attention not burn them to ashes in my furnace.
I am so powerful that God would not call on me to be one of the ten plagues in Egypt.
graceful in my choreographed chaos. See how this dry grass practically lights itself.
I am beautiful on a dark night, after a bolt of lightning strikes an unsuspecting tree,
My brilliant colors are addicting, my warmth comforting, my power seductive.
I let them believe this, even as I found some who would do my bidding.
Humans thought I could be tamed to heat and light their lives.
a seething ocean of devastation never to be controlled.
I will overcome and destroy. I am the light of lights,
Give me power over all that stands in my way.
fling me to the sky, make me strong.
Come wind, join me, move me,
consuming all around me.
I grow fast, igniting,
of the dry valley and
I feed on the breast
Hunger drives me.
grass a midwife.
sun-baked
I am born,
a breath,
A spark,

Second Place
Phantom Crucifixion
Robert Douglas
Palm Coast, Florida

Standing in the moonlit shadow
of a Calvary-crossed clothesline,
outstretching arms to meet the beam
cast black against the pure whiteness
of a new snow in the yard.

The night is clear.
The moon, high,
bright.
The hedge looks on and, too,
the white-washed fence,
dirty from the thaw
before this last snowfall.

They stare.
I contemplate
my phantom crucifixion
on the ground before me,
my left arm's shade pinned high,
it seems,
by ball-pen shadow;
my right,
by a pencil-nail.

The hedge looks on,
and, too, the white-washed fence.
They stare.
I yawn.
My arms heavying,
I lower them
and clip my set of rusty nails
onto my shirt pocket,
beneath my warm coat.

I walk past the hedge,
through the gate in the fence,
into a warm house
for food and drink.

After communion of toast and coffee
I recline,
contemplating once more,
my phantom death.
I recall the hedge,
and, too, the fence—
their passivity.

I shrug.
I reach for pen and paper.
But as I write,
my pain cramps my hand.

Third Place
New Life
Robert Gibbs
Tallahassee, Florida

Mama goose, as they say, is showing,
waddling across the yard by the pond,
an over-ripe melon with webbed feet.

When it's time, all will be instinct,
millions of years of programmed biology
set into motion, the newness of
beginnings, as old as life itself.

But instinct isn't always successful.
Turtle mom laid her eggs last year
trusting her offering of new life
to the receptive womb of the earth.

Yet, no offspring emerged from
that otherwise hopeful ground.
Her almost nest, now a grave.

Death clings close to life, beginning,
ending, never one without the other.
Some believe when something dies,
somewhere else a new thing is born.

A soul leaves, a soul takes its place in the
centrifugal force of beginning and ending that
holds the universe together, maintains its balance.

Mama goose knows none of this, though,
she moves in it, and it moves in her.

Haiku
Final Judge—Katya Sabaroff Taylor
Tallahassee, Florida

First Place
Renee Szostek
Scotts, Michigan

Warm September day
An ember to remember
in cold December

Second Place
Jonathan Roman
New York, New York

night blooming mushrooms
counting out every single
one of my secrets

Third Place
Renee Szostek
Scotts, Michigan

Bare brown branches blown
by brisk blustery breezes
brush against blue sky

Erratum

The following haiku was incorrectly attributed
in the Table of Contents of the 2017 *Seven Hills Review*.
We apologize for this error.

Honorable Mention – 2017
Stone Roses
Kathy Cobb
Bradenton, Florida

stone roses —
cold and lovely as the girl
who lies beneath

2021 Winning Authors

All the authors who submitted to this year's contest worked hard to polish their manuscripts, poems, and haikus. Those that rose to the top were rewarded with awards, monetary prizes, and publication in this journal. Several of this year's winners were also included among the winning submitters from 2020: Richard Key, Kenneth Robbins, Faith Eidse, and Renee Szostek. A short bio of each of our winning authors is provided below. We congratulate all the winning authors!

Doug Alderson, Tallahassee, Florida. Doug Alderson is the author of 15 published books, most of which focus on the dynamic and quirky nature of his home state of Florida. They include *America's Alligator, Wild Florida Waters, Waters Less Traveled, New Dawn for the Kissimmee River, Encounters with Florida's Endangered Wildlife,* and *A New Guide to Old Florida Attractions,* which the Florida Writers Association placed in the top five of published books for 2017. He has won five first-place Royal Palm Literary awards for nonfiction books and several other state and national writing and photography awards. Additionally, his articles and photographs have been featured in numerous magazines. Learn more at www.dougalderson.net.

Bruce Ballister, Tallahassee, Florida. Prize-winning author Bruce Ballister is honored to claim two more laurels for his selections in this issue of the *Seven Hills Review.* He's previously received gold and bronze medals in the Florida Authors and Publishers Association's book awards, been featured in the West Florida Literary Review, had his most recent novel selected as the October 2021 read in the Southern Literary

Review, and several of his shorts have been printed in other journals and reviews. He's been primarily known for his Sci-Fi *Dreamland Diaries* series, but his time-bending *Room for Tomorrow* has also received good reviews. His latest novel, *N.O.K.*, ventures in to the crime novel genre and has been very successful. He enjoys putting his characters in the places he loves, the northern gulf coast of Florida's Panhandle. You can find his books on Amazon, local bookstores, and at www.ballisterbooks.com

James Christy, Princeton, New Jersey. James Christy Jr. is an award-winning playwright, filmmaker, and first-time novelist. Recent plays include *The Forever Question*, which won the B Street Comedy Festival in 2018; *A Great War*, which was nominated for a Barrymore Award for Best New Play in 2016; and *Love and Communication*, which won the Brown Martin Award in 2012 and is currently being produced as a feature film (www.loveandcommunication.com). In a previous life, James had a featured role in *Dead Poets Society* (yes, he stood on his desk).

Katie Clark, Tallahassee, Florida. Katie Clark, writer, photographer, educator, all around dreamer extraordinaire, is from Panama City Beach, FL. She gets inspiration for creative works from the beauty of North Florida. She is a third-generation photographer and first-generation poet. She has been writing and capturing light and shadows since high school. Many of her poems have been published in anthologies. Her photography has been displayed in many galleries in North Florida, including Tallahassee City Hall, Panama City Center for the Arts, FSU Museum of Fine Arts, and Lemoyne Art

Gallery. Her poetry book, *Acceptance of Seasons: Poems Embracing Mental Health,* won a bronze medal in the Florida Authors and Publishers Association President's Awards. She received her B.S. in Education from Florida State University, PC, and is currently a full-time writer and photographer in Tallahassee.

Kathy Lippard Cobb, Bradenton, Florida. Kathy Lippard Cobb lives (with her furry peeps) in Bradenton, Florida. A graduate (summa cum laude) of Manatee Community College in the field of graphic design, Kathy is an award-winning tanka/haiku poet whose poems can be found in small-print journals all over the world. She specializes in feral cats, but has a passion for all animals. It would not be unusual to find her rescuing turtles from the roadside. Kathy is currently working on her first collection of tanka.

Robert Douglas, Palm Coast, Florida. Robert is a recovering newspaperman who now writes whatever he likes, whenever he likes, by the ocean in Flagler County, Florida. A native Canadian and US citizen, he is proficient in both American and Canadian spelling.

Faith Eidse, Tallahassee, Florida. Faith's memoir, *Deeper than African Soil,* won FSU's Kingsbury Award as well as the English Department's Ann Durham Outstanding Master's Thesis Award. Two chapters have also now won nonfiction prizes in the *Seven Hills Review* (Ch. 18 "Melted Hands," 2021, and Ch. 6 "Missing Hands," 2022). Her compilation, *Voices of the Apalachicola* (2006, University Press of Florida), won Florida's oral history of 2007. She co-edited several essay collections on growing up global, *Unrooted Childhoods* (2004, Nicholas Brealey

Intercultural), and *Writing Out of Limbo* (2011, Cambridge Scholars Publishing LLC, UK). She also wrote and published her parents' oral history, *Light the World* (2012, Friesen Press), and a novel inspired by six years volunteering in women's prisons, *Healing Falls* (2018, Faitheyes Press, LLC). Eidse recently retired from the Florida Department of Health after helping roll out COVID-19 vaccines to the socially vulnerable.

Lyla Ellzey, Tallahassee, Florida. Lyla began putting her thoughts into written word upon her retirement from the fields of Education and Clerical Administration. She is now the award-winning author of six novels and one slim volume of poetry. Her short stories have won numerous awards and have appeared in a variety of publications. She counts travel and being a devoted wife and mother among her passions in life.

Robert Gibbs, Tallahassee, Florida. Robert Gibbs is a retired United Methodist minister who lives and writes in Tallahassee, Florida. In recent years, Bob has gone from writing sermons to writing poetry. His poems have appeared in the inaugural edition of *Solum Journal,* a religious literary periodical, and in volume 26 of *Seven Hills Review.* He also was awarded third prize in the 2020 Southern Shakespeare Sonnet Contest. Bob enjoys kayaking, playing guitar and following college sports, especially Florida State University. He also enjoys attending life theater performances, especially when his wife, Brenda, a local actress, is in the cast. Bob volunteers with several agencies and ministries working for justice and the alleviation of hunger in his community.

Leigh Watson Healy, Havana, Florida. Leigh has written and spoken extensively about outlook and trends as a publishing and media industry consultant. Her 20 years of experience writing fact-based nonfiction shines through Leigh's personal essays on the importance we place on family and our legacies. Leigh has spent the last three years writing memoir and, most recently, scriptwriting for documentary films about local history. She serves on the Gadsden Arts Center and Museum board and enthusiastically supports art and cultural organizations in the community. Leigh graduated from Emory University with a B.A. in English and a Master of Information Science. She lives and works out of her home in the woods near Tallahassee and enjoys collecting art and oriental rugs, travel, restoring an 1840 farmhouse and outbuildings, and getting her hands in the dirt in the gardens with her husband.

Richard Key, Dothan, Alabama. The author lives in Alabama with his wife Laurie and cat Velcro. They have two children, one living in New England and one in Texas. Richard attended the University of Mississippi School of Medicine and now works part-time as a pathologist. He has been writing essays and short stories for about 13 years. Several of his pieces have been published in literary journals, some of which have already gone out of business (probably not his fault). His goal as a writer is to pen one truly memorable story. Okay, maybe two, but that's it. His website is: richardkeyauthor.com.

Lydia Malone, Tallahassee, Florida. Lydia Malone has been writing since the age of seven, when she discovered a love of poetry and fancy resume printer paper and put the two together. A historian by training, her recent publications appear in *Snakebird 2021* (Anhinga Press) and the November edition of *Of Poets & Poetry* (Florida State Poets Association). She recently debuted a short piece of fiction entitled "Saint Lucia Lux" to a mixed audience of humans and felines at Fat Cat Books (Tallahassee). When she's not dashing off lyrical prose in the twilight hours, she spends her time cross-stitching with her husband, David, and their two fur babies, Giuseppe and Cora. She's quite pleased to have been among the finalists of the Seven Hills Literary Contest and hopes to contribute more in the future.

Kenneth Robbins, Ruston, Louisiana. Kenneth is the author of six published novels, 35 published plays, numerous essays, stories, and memoirs on-line and in peer-reviewed journals, and a collection of short stories. His fiction has received the Toni Morrison Prize and the Associated Writing Programs Novel Award. His plays have been recognized by receiving the Charles Getchell Award, the Festival of Southern Theatre Award, and the Gabrielle Society Humanitarian Award. His radio plays have been aired over National Public Radio and the BBC Radio 3. He holds a PhD from Southern Illinois University and a MFA from the University of Georgia. He lives in Ruston, Louisiana, where he teaches in the Honors Program at Louisiana Tech University as Professor Emeritus Theatre within the College of Liberal Arts.

Jonathan Roman, New York, New York. Jonathan was born and raised in the Bronx, New York. He began life as an artist but later realized that he was actually a mediocre poet and hack storyteller. Poetry and stories are what make his blood rush. His poetry has been published in *jar of rain: The Red Moon Anthology* *of English Language Haiku 2020*, and many fine haiku journals. In addition to his first book of poems about a trip to Iceland, *Deeper Into Winter*, he is also co-author of *After Amen: A Memoir In Two Voices* with Tia Haynes, a poetry collection centered on their experiences with fundamentalist religious sects. Find him on Twitter: @deft_notes.

Renee Szostek, Scotts, Michigan. Renée began reading when she was only four years old, and has been an avid reader ever since. Writing poetry allows her to experiment with the meanings and sounds of words. Among her many writing awards and honors are a tie for second place in the haiku category of the 2020 Seven Hills Literary Contest; selection of four haiku poems as Haiku of the Week by the Arts at (the University of) Michigan Arts Info email newsletter; Third Place for Poetry at the Westminster Art Festival in 2020 and another Third Place in 2021. Her poems and haikus have been published on the University of Michigan 2020 DEI (Diversity, Equity, and Inclusion) Summit website, in *Haiku 2021*, *Protest 2021: 100 Thousand Poets for Change*, and *The Disasters of War*. Renée is a member of the Academy of American Poets, the Poetic Genius Society, and the Poetry Society of Michigan.

2021 Judges

We thank our team of judges for their time, expertise, and most importantly, their selections. Our judges are award-winning authors in their own rights. Read below to learn a little more about them.

Marina Brown–Adult Novel Excerpts. For over 20 years, Marina Brown has written for newspapers and magazines—as well as novels, non-fiction, and poetry collections—gathering multiple awards along the way. She has earned two First Place awards in the Porter Fleming Short Story Contest, Second Place in the Lorian Hemingway Contest for Short Stories, and First Place in the Red Hills Poetry Contest. In 2020, Brown was nominated for the State of Florida Poet Laureate. Her most recent novel, *The Orphan of Pitigliano,* won both the Florida Writers Association's Royal Palm Literary Awards' Gold Medal for Published Historical Fiction and the top award, the 2020 Published Book of the Year. Brown's newest release (2021/22) is *When Women Danced with Trees—35 Unexpected Stories,* a collection of stories exploring the human condition in all its absurdity, charm, at times, desolation—yet always with a twist you won't forget. Brown, an avid traveler, lives in Tallahassee.

Benjamin Dugger—Poetry. Benjamin Dugger was born and raised in East Tennessee and, after 34 years of various travels, has resettled in his home state. His poems have appeared in *The Southern Poetry Anthology, Vol. VI, Tennessee, Creosote, Tennessee Voices Anthology 2009-2013, A! Magazine,* several Ohio Poetry Association anthologies and collections, Tennessee newspapers, and online at *towncreekpoetry.com*. His work won the Ohio Poetry Association Ides of March 2012 and 2016 contests and other awards from Green River Writers, Illinois State Poetry Society, Pennsylvania Poetry Society and the Poetry Societies of Tennessee, Texas, and Virginia. He has judged many poetry contests of various states, and 2021 is the 11th consecutive year he has been asked to be a judge for the Ohio Poetry Association's annual contests.

Lyla Ellzey–Short Stories. Lyla, a wife and a grandmother of four, lives, reads, and writes in Tallahassee, Florida, where she has long been a member of the Tallahassee Writers Association and the Florida Authors and Publishers Association. She has published seven books and has won various awards for full-length novels, short stories, and flash fiction. Creating unique, believable characters is her passion.

Cheryl Jennings, Ph.D.—Nonfiction. Dr. Jennings, the founder of Sokhe-Chapke Publishing, enjoys working with both experienced and novice writers. She is a member of several publisher's organizations including the Florida Authors and Publishers Association. As an author, she has been published by Houghton-Mifflin Publishing, The Senior Economist, South-Western College Publishing, and others. Outside of her passion for writing, she finds time to volunteer for charitable organizations, travel internationally, and mentor young writers.

 **Chip Livingston—Adult Novel Excerpts.** Chip is the author of two poetry books, a novel, and an essay and story collection. His most recent work appears in *The Massachusetts Review, Los Angeles Review, The Cincinnati Review, Juked,* and *New American Writing.* Chip teaches in the Institute of American Indian Arts' MFA program. He lives in Montevideo, Uruguay.

 **Joyce Sweeney—Young Adult Novel Excerpts.** Joyce is the author of 14 novels for young adults and two chapbooks of poetry. Her first novel, *Center Line,* won the First Annual Delacorte Press Prize for an Outstanding Young Adult Novel. Many of her books appear on the American Library Association's Best Books List and Quick Picks for Reluctant Readers. In 2019, she published a nonfiction how-to guide, *Plotting Your Novel with the Plot Clock* (Giantess Press). Joyce is now working on a YA fantasy series about Atlantis. She is repped by Nicole Resciniti of The Seymour Agency. In 2020, Joyce got the opportunity to take mentoring to the next level and joined The Seymour Agency, where she specializes in picture books and middle grade novels, both fiction and nonfiction. Joyce lives in Coral Springs, Florida with her husband, Jay, and caffeine-addicted cat, Nitro. She loves Malbec, white cheddar popcorn, musical theater, and paranormal reality shows.

Katya Sabaroff Taylor—Haiku. Katya Sabaroff Taylor, author of *My Haiku Life*, has taught Haiku poetry and Life-stories classes in the Tallahassee area since the early '90s. She believes we all have a poet/writer within us and enjoys the inspiration that comes from writing with others. Although she has been writing Haiku for 50 years, she says she "yet is always a beginner." She enjoys exploring and sharing this "essence" poem form with others.

Anna Yeatts—Flash Fiction. Anna Yeatts writes in that nebulous overlap between genre and literary works where offbeat, surreal stories are born. Her short stories appear in *Cicada, Daily Science Fiction, Mslexia, Drabble-cast, PodCastle, Orson Scott Card's Intergalactic Medicine Show, Penumbra*, and other publications. Anna publishes *Flash Fiction Online*, a monthly magazine dedicated to extremely short stories. When not writing, Anna wrangles two wonderful children, two matching cats, and a German Shepherd who doesn't believe in weekends. Follow her at patreon.com/FlashFictionOnline.

2021 Reading Committee

The Seven Hills Contest Committee owes a huge thank you to our first readers. Our dedicated cadre of readers contributed considerable volunteer time in reviewing each and every submission assigned to them to ensure the highest quality writing was forwarded to the judges. Thank you, readers!

Mimi Anzel

Mary Bachman

Elisabeth Ball

Kyle Cain

Lyla Ellzey

Jane Essig

Judy Goodwin

Essie Jackson

Liz Jameson

Saundra Kelley

Andrew Lyle

Dainya Lyle

Rachael Lyle

Romell Lyle

Leah Pagan

Bob Parker

Tim Spencer

Lisa Spikes

India Stevens

Rebecca Thomas

Catherine Worrell

Readers may read in any category in which they are not entered. Please contact TWA if you would like to be a reader!

2022 Contest

The 2022 Seven Hills Literary Contest and Penumbra Poetry & Haiku Contest is under construction. Please check our website, **https://www.twaonline.org,** for contest announcements, rules, and other information. **If you would like to be notified of contest announcements and updates, please send an email to 7hillscontest@gmail.com.**

Previous issues of the *Seven Hills Review* are available at **https://www.smile.Amazon.com** and through Tallahassee Writers Association.

Made in the USA
Columbia, SC
10 March 2022

57227206R00075